Sandra Lee

semi-homemade

Cocktail Time

This book belongs to:

_____

Thank you to Jon, Jennifer, Tori, Dave, Ken, Lisa, Joe & Nancee

This book is printed on acid-free paper.

Published by John Wiley & Sons, Inc., Hoboken, New Jersey, in partnership with SL Books.

Published simultaneously in Canada.

Cover photo by George Lange; selected author photos by Jill Lotenberg.

For general information on our other products and services or for technical support, please contact our Customer Care Department within the United States at (800) 762-2974, outside the United States at (317) 572-3993, or fax (317) 572-4002.

Wiley also publishes its books in a variety of electronic formats. Some content that appears in print may not be available in electronic books. For more information about Wiley products, visit our web site at www.wiley.com.

Library of Congress Cataloging-in-Publication Data:
Lee, Sandra, 1966-
  Semi-homemade cocktail time / Sandra Lee.
       p. cm.
Includes index.
ISBN 978-0-470-55487-6 (pbk.)
1. Cocktails. 2. Appetizers. 3. Quick and easy cookery. I. Title.
TX951.L435 2009
641.8'74--dc22

                                          2009034011

Printed in the United States of America.

10 9 8 7 6 5 4 3 2 1

SL BOOKS
sandralee.com

WILEY
John Wiley & Sons, Inc.

table of contents

blue cosmo ten midori passion
fruit martini peach cîroc
blue ocean ten blue lagoon
heirloom sangria mixed-berry
daiquiri florence fizzy peachy
margarita blue seafoam blue
hawaiian blue cosmo ten midori
passion fruit martini peach
drop cîroc blue ocean ten blue
lagoon heirloom sangria mixed
blue cosmo ten midori passion
fruit martini peach drop
blue ocean ten blue lagoon

cheers from sandra

Cheers to you, dear friends. You are the reason I created this book. At every book signing, every party, every TV show appearance, and even when I simply walk through the grocery store, I'm always asked, "When are you going to do a cocktail book?" I'm happy to say it's *Cocktail Time*. It's *Cocktail Time* for a cause—and not just our "own" cause. This book is to be used to help celebrate each and every day of our lives while making the world a better place.

Cocktailing for a Cause is a philanthropic initiative where anyone can make a difference. Host a special fundraising "cocktail time" party with your friends and family, and donate the proceeds to a charity. I always contribute to causes near to my heart and I do my best to lead by example, so in purchasing this book please know that you are already making a difference. Proceeds from this book are being donated to help support two worthy charities: Water for Life and Malaria No More.

Water for Life is a series of projects supported by the Diageo Foundation. Diageo is the company that gives us many of the drinks we love—Baileys Irish Cream, Tanqueray Gin, José Cuervo Tequila, Smirnoff's Pomegranate Martini and Tuscan Lemonade, as well as Godiva liqueurs and many more. In addition to aiding environmental conservation, Water of Life has provided access to clean drinking water to more than 3.2 million people in 10 countries.

I am also proud that this book is supporting Malaria No More. This non-profit organization is committed to ending unnecessary deaths from malaria. Malaria No More mixes breakthrough marketing with media events to place malaria at the top of the agenda for policymakers and the public.

Choose a cause close to your heart, and together we can make the world a better place and have fun doing so. Use my cocktail recipes to host your own party and raise your glass and awareness for the causes that have special meaning to you.

I send to you a warm hug along with some sisterly advice—remember to drink responsibly.

Cheers to you and yours,
Sandra Lee

Aquamarine Cocktail In a pitcher combine 4 ounces blue curaçao liqueur, 4 ounces tequila, *Jose Cuervo Especial*, and two 12-ounce cans lemon-lime soda. Serve over ice. Makes 4 drinks.

haute hosting

The Perfect Party: A cocktail party is an ideal (and stylish!) way for a busy hostess to entertain anyone, including friends, family, neighbors, or business associates. It doesn't require the preparation and planning that a full-scale, sit-down dinner party does and—because of the mix-and-mingle nature of a cocktail party—it creates a casual atmosphere in which a combination of very different people can come together and feel relaxed and comfortable.

Stock Up: In addition to a well-stocked bar (see "Build a Bar," pages 8–9), you need to keep a few crucial things in mind when planning a cocktail party. First, be sure you have plenty of ice. You'll need it to chill bottles of wine, Champagne, or prosecco, as well as to serve drinks. Plan for about 1 pound of ice per guest. It's also a good idea to have twice as many glasses as guests—that is, two clean glasses per guest.

Eat, Drink, Be Merry: Cocktail parties are about more than just the drinks. You always want to serve food—not just because a cocktail or glass of wine and something to nibble tastes delicious together, but also because it's always a good idea to have food in your stomach when drinking alcohol.

Celebrate Responsibly: Offer soft drinks, fruit juices, water, or other nonalcoholic drinks. Ensure that food is available, and never serve more than one drink at a time to your guests. If any of your guests has too much to drink, don't allow them to drive—call them a cab.

build a bar

The Basics: The foundation of any well-stocked bar is the selection of spirits that are used as the basis of so many drinks. The essentials include tequila, rum, gin, vodka, and whiskey. With just these five spirits—plus mixers such as juices, sodas, simple syrup, bitters, and tonic—you can make hundreds of cocktails. If you want to expand your bar, add flavored spirits, sweet and dry vermouth, orange liqueur, or Irish cream liqueur.

The Toolbox: It takes very little equipment to become a master mixologist. The most essential tool is a cocktail shaker for combining and quick-chilling liquids. The most common type, made of stainless steel, is widely available and inexpensive. The other must-have is a jigger for measuring. Most have two ends—a 1½-ounce side (a shot) and a 1-ounce side (a pony).

Glamour in a Glass: Cocktails look best served in the perfect glass. Classic shapes to consider stocking in your bar include martini, rocks (or old-fashioned), collins, margarita, shot glasses, and tall fluted glasses for drinks made with sparkling wines.

THE CÎROC DIDDY

1½ ounces vodka, *Cîroc®*

3 ounces lemonade

Combine vodka, lemonade, and ice in a cocktail shaker. Shake and strain into glass.

"The Official Drink of Summer"

wise on wine

Wine Types: Although specific varieties and vintages of wines have very specific flavors, some generalizations can be made. Red wines have notes of spice, smoke, dark berries or cherries, coffee, and cocoa. White wines often have the flavors of peaches, herbs, tropical fruits, and—if they are aged in oak—spice or vanilla. When you're hosting a party, it's good to have a few varieties of both red and white wines on hand to please every palate. Popular reds include cabernet sauvignon, merlot, pinot noir, zinfandel, and syrah. Popular whites include chardonnay, pinot grigio, sauvignon blanc, and riesling.

Mulled or Mixed: Wine poured right from the bottle is wonderful all on its own, but it can also be the starring ingredient in all kinds of drinks, both hot and cold. Consider a spicy, warming mulled wine or wassail on a cold fall or winter night—or a refreshing fruited sangria for a summer party.

What to Eat with Wine: Cheese is the go-to accompaniment with wine. Strong, long-aged cheeses stand up well to hearty reds, while fresh, milder cheeses pair well with lighter whites. Fruits and desserts are always delicious—and chocolate with spicy red wine is classic.

easy edibles

Dress It Up: The effect of garnishing a cocktail is a bit like adding the right jewelry to a great dress—it makes a beautiful thing that much more beautiful. Garnishes can be as simple as a sprig of fresh mint, a sugared rim, or a slice of fresh fruit (or whole strawberry) dropped into the bottom of the glass or draped on the rim. Fresh fruits such as cranberries, raspberries, blueberries, or kumquats speared on a pretty swizzle stick look lovely too.

Picks and Swizzle Sticks: Aside from a good sharp paring knife and chef's knife, making garnishes doesn't require any particular tools. It is nice to have a set (or two) of cocktail picks and swizzle sticks. Picks are perfect for spearing olives or cocktail onions, while swizzle sticks can hold a neat line of berries or other small fruits.

Food with Flair: When it comes to pairing up cocktails and food, think creatively. A mix of appetizers—hot and cold, finger foods, dips, and spreads—is always welcome, but don't limit yourself. Consider side dishes such as vegetable salads or hot dishes that guests can eat with their fingers or with a cocktail fork. Top things off with a few bites of dessert and something sweet to sip.

january

buca-cino orange margarita
coconut ginger mojito pom
blanco champagne sabayon
cranberry punch pizazz
cream twist pb&j martini
irish grasshopper buca-cino
coconut ginger mojito pom
blanco champagne sabayon
cranberry punch pizazz
cream twist pb&j martini

POM BLANCO

Makes 1 drink

1½	ounces tequila, *Don Julio® Blanco*
¾	ounce pomegranate juice
½	ounce lime juice
	Splash simple syrup
	Splash soda water
	Cranberry swizzle stick

In a cocktail shaker filled with ice, combine tequila, pomegranate juice, lime juice, and simple syrup. Shake vigorously until very cold. Strain into a glass. Top with a splash of soda water. Garnish with a cranberry swizzle stick.

CHIANTI-POACHED PEARS

Prep 10 minutes **Cook** 6 hours (Low) **Makes** 6 servings

4	underripe pears, peeled
1	medium orange, sliced
2	tablespoons mulling spices, *Morton & Bassett®*
1	bottle (750-milliliter) Chianti, *Stella di Notte®*
1	cup packed brown sugar, *Domino®/C&H®*
	Orange juice or water (optional)

1. Cut each pear in half and use a melon baller to remove core. Place pear halves in a 4- to 5-quart slow cooker. Add orange slices and mulling spices. In a bowl, stir together Chianti and brown sugar; pour over pears. Add orange juice or water (optional).

2. Cover slow cooker and cook on Low heat setting for 6 to 8 hours or until pears can be easily pierced with a fork.

CHAMPAGNE SABAYON

Makes 6 drinks

1¼	cups extra-dry Champagne, *Moët & Chandon*®
¼	cup honey
1	package (16-ounce) frozen mixed berries, thawed
3	teaspoons grated orange zest
¼	cup fresh orange juice
1	package (12.3-ounce) silken extra-firm tofu
	Orange zest curls (optional)

In a glass measuring cup, combine ½ cup of the Champagne and 2 tablespoons of the honey, stirring until honey dissolves. In a small bowl, pour Champagne over berries. Stir 2 teaspoons of the orange zest and the orange juice into berry mixture. Let stand at room temperature for 30 minutes to 1 hour. For the Champagne Sabayon, place remaining ¾ cup Champagne into blender. Add tofu, the remaining 2 tablespoons honey, and the remaining 1 teaspoon orange zest. Cover and blend on high until smooth. Chill in refrigerator until ready to serve. To serve, divide berry mixture among 6 champagne flutes. Top with Champagne Sabayon. Garnish with orange zest curls (optional).

SHRIMP PUFFS WITH ORANGE-MUSTARD DIPPING SAUCE

Prep 20 minutes   **Cook** 2 minutes per batch   **Makes** 20 puffs

FOR SHRIMP PUFFS

1	package (6-ounce) rice stick noodles (mai fun), *China Sea*®
1	pound medium shrimp, peeled and deveined
⅓	cup sliced water chestnuts, *Dynasty*®
1	tablespoon cornstarch
1	tablespoon ponzu sauce, *Kikkoman*®
1	egg white
1	teaspoon Szechwan seasoning, *Spice Islands*®
1	teaspoon bottled minced ginger, *Christopher Ranch*®
1	teaspoon bottled crushed garlic, *Christopher Ranch*®
¼	teaspoon dark sesame oil, *Dynasty*®
	Peanut oil

FOR ORANGE-MUSTARD DIPPING SAUCE

½	cup orange marmalade, *Knott's Berry Farm*®
¼	cup pineapple juice, *Dole*®
1	tablespoon Chinese dry mustard, *Sun Luck*®
1	teaspoon low-sodium soy sauce, *Kikkoman*®
½	teaspoon bottled minced ginger, *Christopher Ranch*®

1. For Shrimp Puffs: Coarsely chop rice stick noodles into ½-inch lengths. Transfer chopped noodles to a shallow bowl.

2. In a food processor, combine shrimp, water chestnuts, cornstarch, ponzu sauce, egg white, Szechwan seasoning, ginger, garlic, and sesame oil. Cover and pulse until finely chopped but not pureed. Form mixture into 1-inch balls, using about 2 tablespoons. Roll shrimp balls in chopped noodles.

3. In a medium or large saucepan, heat 1 inch peanut oil over medium to medium-high heat until temperature reaches 375 degrees F. Fry shrimp balls, several at a time, for 2 to 3 minutes or until golden brown. Remove shrimp balls using a slotted spoon or wire strainer. Drain on paper towels. Keep warm in a 300 degrees F oven while cooking remaining shrimp balls. Serve warm.

4. For Orange-Mustard Dipping Sauce: In a small bowl, combine marmalade, pineapple juice, mustard, soy sauce, and ginger. Serve with Shrimp Puffs.

ORANGE MARGARITA

Makes 1 drink

1½ ounces tequila, *Jose Cuervo Especial*®
1 ounce blood orange mixer, *Stirrings*®
¼ ounce blood orange bitters, *Stirrings*®
  Ice cubes

In a cocktail shaker, combine tequila, blood orange mixer, and blood orange bitters. Add ice; cover and shake until very cold. Strain into a chilled glass.

CHIVE-ROASTED POTATOES WITH CAVIAR

Prep 20 minutes   **Roast** 35 minutes   **Makes** 30 pieces

2	pounds new red potatoes and/or purple potatoes
2	tablespoons extra virgin olive oil, *Bertolli®*
2	tablespoons finely chopped fresh chives
½	teaspoon kosher salt
¼	teaspoon ground black pepper
½	cup sour cream
1	teaspoon prepared horseradish
1	jar (2-ounce) caviar,* *Romanoff®*

1. Preheat oven to 400 degrees F. Line baking sheet with parchment paper.

2. Wash and dry potatoes. Slice into ½-inch rounds.

3. Place potatoes in a medium bowl and drizzle with olive oil. Add chopped chives, salt, and pepper; toss to coat.

4. Arrange potatoes on parchment-lined baking sheet. Roast in oven for 35 to 40 minutes or until potatoes are cooked through. Set aside to cool.

5. Meanwhile, in a small bowl, stir together sour cream and horseradish. Cover and chill until serving time.

6. To assemble, top chive-roasted potatoes with sour cream mixture. With a plastic spoon,* add a small amount of caviar. Serve at room temperature.

*Note: Do not use a metal spoon for caviar.

COCONUT GINGER MOJITO

Makes 1 drink

	Ice cubes
1½	ounces mojito drink mix, *Stirrings®*
1½	ounces coconut rum, *Captain Morgan Parrot Bay®* *Coconut*
1	splash ginger ale
	Fresh mint sprig

Fill short glass with ice. Pour in mojito mix and rum. Top with ginger ale. Stir gently and garnish with fresh mint.

CREAM TWIST

Makes 1 drink

2	ounces Irish cream liqueur, *Baileys®*
½	ounce vanilla flavored vodka, *Smirnoff®*
	Ice cubes

In a cocktail shaker, combine Irish cream and vodka. Add ice; cover and shake until very cold. Strain into a chilled martini glass.

FIG AND PORT TARTLETS

Prep 15 minutes   **Cook** 6 minutes   **Makes** 15 tartlets

1	jar (12-ounce) royal fig preserves, *St. Dalfour®*
¼	cup port
2	cups whipping cream
3	tablespoons granulated sugar, *Domino®/C&H®*
¼	teaspoon cinnamon extract, *McCormick®*
1	package (2.1-ounce) baked miniature phyllo dough shells, *Athens®*
	Ground cinnamon, *McCormick®*
	Powdered sugar, *Domino®/C&H®*

1. In a saucepan, over medium heat, heat preserves and port, about 6 minutes or until mixture thickens. Remove from heat; set aside.

2. In a chilled mixing bowl, beat whipping cream, sugar, and cinnamon extract with an electric mixer on medium speed until stiff peaks form. Transfer whipped cream mixture to a large zip-top plastic bag. Snip ½ inch off one corner of the bag. Fill each shell with about 1 tablespoon of fig mixture. Pipe whipped cream on top. Garnish with a dusting of ground cinnamon and powdered sugar.

IRISH GRASSHOPPER

Makes I drink

2   **ounces Irish cream liqueur,** *Baileys*®

½   **ounce half-and-half**

¼   **ounce chocolate liqueur,** *Godiva*®

¼   **ounce crème de menthe**

      Ice cubes

In a cocktail shaker, combine Irish cream, half-and-half, chocolate liqueur, and crème de menthe. Add ice; cover and shake until very cold. Fill a glass with additional ice. Strain into glass.

HOT DATES

Prep 15 minutes **Soak** 15 minutes
Broil 3 minutes **Makes** 16 dates

1	package (8-ounce) pitted dates, *Sunsweet*®
1	can (15-ounce) pineapple chunks, drained, *Del Monte*®
1	package (16-ounce) bacon, slices cut in half, *Hormel*®

1. Preheat the broiler.

2. Soak wooden toothpicks in water about 15 minutes.

3. Cut a slit in each date; stuff a pineapple chunk into each slit. Wrap each date with a half-slice bacon; secure with a soaked toothpick.

4. Place bacon-wrapped dates on a baking sheet. Broil dates 6 inches from the heat for 3 to 5 minutes or until bacon is crisp on all sides, turning occasionally. Drain on paper towels. Serve warm.

CRANBERRY PUNCH PIZZAZZ

Prep 10 minutes **Cook** 2 hours (High) or 4 hours (Low)
Makes 18 drinks

8	whole cardamom pods
16	inches stick cinnamon, broken
12	whole cloves
1	can (11.5- or 12-ounce) frozen cranberry juice concentrate
	Water
4	cups Merlot, *Beaulieu Vineyard*®
⅓	cup honey
	Fresh cranberries
	Orange slices

For spice bag, cut a 6-inch square from a double thickness of 100-percent-cotton cheesecloth. Pinch cardamom pods to break. Center the cardamom, cinnamon, and cloves on the cheesecloth square. Bring up the corners and tie closed with clean kitchen string. Set aside. In a 3½- to 6-quart slow cooker, mix cranberry juice concentrate with water according to the directions on the can. Stir in wine and honey. Add spice bag. Cover and cook on Low heat setting for 4 to 6 hours or on High heat setting for 2 to 2½ hours. Remove and discard spice bag. Ladle punch into glasses. Garnish with cranberries and orange slices.

PB&J MARTINI

Makes I drink

Ice cubes

I   **ounce raspberry flavored vodka,
Smirnoff®**

I½ **ounces hazelnut liqueur**

I½ **ounces purple grape juice**

Fresh raspberries

Fill cocktail shaker with ice. Add all ingredients
and shake vigorously. Strain into a chilled martini
glass. Garnish with raspberries.

BUCA-CINO

Makes 1 drink

1	**ounce half-and-half**
1	**ounce milk**
¾	**ounce sambuca,** *Romana Sambuca®*
½	**ounce gin,** *Tanqueray®*
	Ice cubes

In a cocktail shaker, combine half-and-half, milk, sambuca, and gin. Add ice; cover and shake until very cold. Strain into a chilled martini glass.

MINI CHICKEN POTPIES

Prep 25 minutes   **Bake** 25 minutes   **Makes** 12 potpies

⅓	**cup chicken broth,** *Swanson®*
2	**cans (10 ounces each) chicken breast, drained,** *Hormel®*
8	**ounces frozen mixed vegetables (corn, peas, carrots)**
½	**can (10.75-ounce) condensed cream of celery soup,** *Campbell's®*
1	**tablespoon garlic-herb seasoning blend,** *McCormick®*
	Ground black pepper
5	**sheets frozen phyllo dough, thawed,** *Athens Foods®*
¼	**cup (½ stick) butter, melted**

1. Preheat oven to 375 degrees F. Line a baking sheet with parchment paper. Arrange 12 ovensafe espresso (demitasse) cups about 2 inches apart on baking sheet; set aside.

2. In a medium saucepan, over medium heat, heat broth. Add chicken and frozen vegetables. Cook, covered, for 15 minutes. Add soup and seasoning blend. Cook and stir for another 5 minutes. Season to taste with pepper. Fill each cup with 1 heaping tablespoon of chicken mixture.

3. Lay out 1 sheet of phyllo dough (keep remaining phyllo covered with plastic wrap to prevent it from drying out). Brush phyllo with butter. Top with another sheet of phyllo. Brush phyllo with butter. Repeat brushing with butter and layering with 3 more sheets of phyllo (using 5 sheets for one stack). Cut stack in thirds lengthwise. Cut crosswise into fourths. There should be a total of 12 rectangles. Top each cup with a phyllo rectangle and fold corners toward sides of cups.

4. Bake about 25 minutes or until phyllo turns golden brown and sheets puff up slightly. Serve warm.

february

blood orange bellini godiva
polar freeze orange paradise
martini baileys hot cocoa
cranberry grand irish coffee
bloody mary orange crusier
raspberry cosmo lemontini
flirtini moulin rouge blood
orange bellini godiva polar
freeze raspberry cosmo
bloody mary orange crusier

BLOOD ORANGE BELLINI

Makes 1 drink

- 1   ounce blood orange mixer, *Stirrings®*
- 4   ounces sparkling wine, *Chandon®*

In a chilled Champagne flute, combine blood orange mixer and sparkling wine. Stir gently; serve.

BALSAMIC ROASTED TOMATOES

Prep 5 minutes   **Roast** 10 minutes   **Makes** 4 servings

- 4   medium roma tomatoes, sliced
- 2   tablespoons light balsamic vinaigrette, *Newman's Own®*
- 1   tablespoon grated Parmesan cheese, *DiGiorno®*
- 1   tablespoon chopped fresh basil

1. Preheat oven to 400 degrees F. Line a rimmed baking pan with aluminum foil. Place tomato slices, on baking sheet. Sprinkle with balsamic vinaigrette, Parmesan, and basil. Roast for 10 to 12 minutes or until tomatoes are heated through.

CRANBERRY GRAND

Makes 1 drink

2	**ounces grapefruit juice**
1½	**ounces cranberry flavored vodka, *Smirnoff*®**
¼	**ounce grenadine**
¼	**ounce lime juice**
	Ice cubes
	Cranberries

In a cocktail shaker, combine grapefruit juice, vodka, grenadine, and lime juice. Add ice; cover and shake until very cold. Strain into a chilled glass. Garnish with cranberries.

BAILEYS HOT COCOA

Makes I drink

I	cup hot cocoa, *Hershey's®*
3½	ounces Irish cream liqueur, *Baileys®*
I½	ounces espresso Thai iced tea
I	ounce milk

In a mug, combine hot cocoa, liqueur, iced tea, and milk. Serve warm.

PÂTÉ "POP TARTS"

Prep 25 minutes　**Bake** 20 minutes　**Makes** 4 "pop tarts"

	No-stick cooking spray, *Pam®*
I	package (6.5-ounce) pizza crust mix, *Betty Crocker®*
¼	teaspoon ground black pepper
¼	cup cognac
¼	cup water
4	ounces foie gras mousse pâté, *D'Artagnan®*
I	egg, lightly beaten
I	tablespoon half-and-half

1. Preheat oven to 375 degrees F. Coat a baking sheet with cooking spray. In a bowl, combine crust mix and pepper. In a microwave-safe bowl, combine cognac and water. Heat on high heat setting (100% power) for 30 seconds; stir into crust mixture.

2. On a floured surface, roll out dough to ⅛ inch thick. Cut out eight 5x3-inch rectangles. Spread I tablespoon pâté onto 4 rectangles, leaving a ¼-inch border. Brush border with egg; top with remaining rectangles. Use fork to crimp edges and prick top of dough. Beat remaining egg with half-in-half and brush top of dough. Bake for 20 minutes or until golden brown. Serve warm.

IRISH COFFEE

Makes 1 drink

3   ounces fresh brewed coffee

1   ounce Irish whiskey, *Bushmills® Original*

1   ounce sugar syrup

Whipped cream

In a mug, combine coffee, whiskey, and sugar syrup. Top with whipped cream.

BLOODY MARY

Makes 1 drink

3	ounces tomato juice
1	ounce vodka, *Smirnoff No. 21™*
½	ounce lemon juice
2	dashes red hot pepper sauce
2	dashes green hot pepper sauce
	Dash Worcestershire sauce
	Salt
	Ice cubes
	Half-slice lemon, pickled hot pepper

In a large glass, combine tomato juice, vodka, lemon juice, red hot sauce, green hot sauce, a pinch of *salt* and *black pepper,* and the Worcestershire sauce. Pour into another large glass. Pour back and forth between the two glasses. Wet the rim of a chilled glass with water; dip rim in salt. Fill glass with ice; strain mixture into glass. Garnish with lemon and pickled hot pepper.

MINI BISCUIT PIZZAS

Prep 25 minutes   **Bake** 12 minutes   **Makes** 24 pizzas

3	packages (16.3 ounces each) refrigerated prepared buttermilk biscuit dough, *Pillsbury® Grands!®*
	No-stick cooking spray, *Pam®*
1	cup chopped onion
1	package (3-ounce) thinly sliced prosciutto, chopped, *Citterio®*
1	cup purchased traditional tomato sauce, *Ragu®*
6	large fresh mushrooms, sliced
1	cup shredded pizza-blend cheese, *Sargento®*
	Fresh basil leaves

1. Bake biscuits according to package instructions. Cool biscuits on wire racks.

2. Coat a baking sheet with cooking spray. Split biscuits in half and arrange, split sides up, on baking sheet. Set aside. Preheat oven to 400 degrees F.

3. In a bowl, combine onion and prosciutto. In another bowl, combine tomato sauce and mushrooms. Spread tomato mixture over biscuit halves. Sprinkle with cheese. Top with onion mixture. Bake about 12 minutes or until topping is golden brown. Garnish with basil. Serve warm.

RASPBERRY COSMO

Makes 1 drink

1	ounce raspberry flavored vodka, *Smirnoff®*
½	ounce orange liqueur, *Grand Marnier®*
1	splash lime juice
1	splash cranberry juice
	Ice cubes

In a cocktail shaker, combine vodka, orange liqueur, lime juice, and cranberry juice. Add ice; cover and shake until very cold. Strain into a chilled glass.

CHILE BEEF SATAY

Prep 30 minutes   **Marinate** 2 to 24 hours   **Makes** 5 or 6 servings

FOR BEEF SATAY

1¼	pounds boneless beef sirloin steak
1	cup lower-sodium beef broth, *Swanson®*
3	tablespoons white vinegar, *Heinz®*
3	tablespoons soy sauce, *Kikkoman®*
1	tablespoon chile-garlic sauce, *Lee Kum Kee®*

FOR SWEET CHILE DIPPING SAUCE

1½	cups sugar, *Domino®/C&H®*
½	cup white vinegar, *Heinz®*
1	tablespoon salt-free Thai seasoning, *The Spice Hunter®*
1	tablespoon chile-garlic sauce, *Lee Kum Kee®*
1	teaspoon salt
	Sesame seeds (optional)

1. Cut beef across the grain into ¼-inch-thick slices. Place in a large zip-top plastic bag. For marinade, in a small bowl, combine beef broth, vinegar, soy sauce, and chile-garlic sauce. Pour into bag with beef. Squeeze out air and seal. Gently massage to combine ingredients. Marinate in the refrigerator for at least 2 hours or overnight.

2. Soak 6-inch wooden skewers in water for at least 1 hour.

3. For Sweet Chile Dipping Sauce: In a medium saucepan, combine sugar, vinegar, Thai seasoning, chile-garlic sauce, and salt. Bring to a boil over medium-high heat; reduce heat. Simmer for 5 to 10 minutes or until sugar is dissolved, stirring occasionally. Transfer to a bowl and cool.

4. Remove beef from the marinade; discard marinade. Drain skewers. Thread beef, accordion style, onto skewers. Preheat broiler. Place skewers on a wire rack over a foil-lined baking sheet or broiler pan. Broil 6 to 8 inches from heat for 4 to 6 minutes or until beef is cooked through, turning halfway through broiling. Sprinkle with sesame seeds (optional). Serve with dipping sauce.

GODIVA POLAR FREEZE

Makes 1 drink

1   ounce white chocolate liqueur, *Godiva®*
1   ounce peppermint schnapps,
      Rumple Minze®
      Ground nutmeg, white chocolate bar

In a glass, combine white chocolate liqueur and peppermint schnapps. Sprinkle with nutmeg. Garnish with white chocolate bar.

LEMONTINI

Makes 1 drink

1½   ounces citrus vodka, *Ketel One Citroen®*
1   ounce Fresh Lemon Sour
         (see recipe, below)
1   tablespoon sugar
1   splash sugar syrup
       Ice cubes
       Plum slice

In a cocktail shaker, combine vodka, Fresh Lemon Sour, sugar, and sugar syrup. Add ice; cover and shake until very cold. Strain into prepared glass. Garnish with plum slice. For the Fresh Lemon Sour: In a small container, combine 4 ounces lemon juice, 2 ounces sugar syrup, and ½ ounce water. Cover and store in the refrigerator.

FLIRTINI

Makes 1 drink

1	ounce citrus flavored vodka, *Smirnoff®*
¾	ounce unsweetened pineapple juice
¾	ounce cranberry juice
½	ounce coconut rum, *Captain Morgan Parrot Bay® Coconut*
	Splash sweet-and-sour mix
	Ice cubes, fresh coconut pieces, fresh cranberries

In a cocktail shaker, combine vodka, pineapple juice, cranberry juice, rum, and sweet-and-sour mix. Add ice; cover and shake until very cold. Strain into a chilled martini glass. Garnish with coconut and cranberries.

HOT CRAB RANGOON DIP

Prep 10 minutes   **Cook** 2 hours (Low)   **Makes** 12 servings

2	packages (8 ounces each) cream cheese, cut into cubes, *Philadelphia®*
2	cans (6 ounces each) crabmeat, drained, flaked, and cartilage removed, *Crown Prince®*
1	can (10.75-ounce) condensed cream of shrimp soup, *Campbell's®*
1	green onion, finely chopped
2	teaspoons lemon juice, *ReaLemon®*
2	teaspoons soy sauce, *Kikkoman®*
1	teaspoon Worcestershire sauce, *Lea & Perrins®*

1. In a 3- to 4-quart slow cooker, combine cream cheese, crabmeat, shrimp soup, green onion, lemon juice, soy sauce, and Worcestershire sauce. Cover and cook on Low heat setting for 2 to 3 hours. Serve.

ORANGE CRUISER

Makes 1 drink

4	ounces sweet-and-sour mix
1¼	ounces bourbon, *Bulleit®*
¾	ounce mint syrup
¾	ounce pineapple syrup
	Ice cubes, orange twist

In a cocktail shaker, combine sweet-and-sour mix, bourbon, mint syrup, and pineapple syrup. Add ice; cover and shake until very cold. Strain into chilled glass. Garnish with orange twist.

MOULIN ROUGE

Makes 1 drink

> 1½ **ounces white rum, *Oronoco*®**
> 1½ **ounces pomegranate juice**
>   **Splash orange liqueur, *Grand Marnier*®**
>   **Ice cubes, fresh orange wedges, fresh raspberries**

In a cocktail shaker, combine rum, pomegranate juice, and orange liqueur. Add ice; cover and shake until very cold. Strain into a chilled glass. Garnish with orange wedges and raspberries.

PARADISE MARTINI

Makes 1 drink

	Ice cubes
1	ounce vodka, *Cîroc®*
1	tablespoon cold water
½	ounce crème de cassis
½	ounce amaretto
1	lime wedge
	Maraschino cherry

Fill a cocktail shaker with ice. Add vodka, cold water, crème de cassis, and amaretto. Squeeze in lime juice. Cover and shake vigorously. Strain into chilled martini glass. Garnish with cherry.

GINGER-GARLIC SHRIMP

Prep 10 minutes   **Cook** 11 minutes   **Makes** 8 servings

1	teaspoon ground ginger, *McCormick®*
2	teaspoons Szechwan seasoning, *Spice Islands®*
1¼	pounds fresh large shrimp, peeled and deveined (leave tails intact if desired)
2	tablespoons canola oil
½	cup chicken broth
¼	cup ginger preserves, *Robertson's®*
¼	cup frozen raspberries, thawed
2	tablespoons rice wine vinegar
2	teaspoons bottled crushed garlic, *Christopher Ranch®*

1. In a small bowl, stir together ground ginger and Szechwan seasoning. Sprinkle ginger mixture evenly over both sides of the shrimp; set aside.

2. In a large skillet, heat oil over medium-high heat. Add shrimp; cook 6 minutes or until cooked through, turning once halfway through cooking. Transfer to a serving plate; cover and set aside.

3. Carefully add chicken broth to hot skillet. To deglaze skillet, scrape brown bits from the bottom. Add ginger preserves; stir until melted. Stir in raspberries, rice wine vinegar, and garlic. Bring to a boil; reduce heat. Simmer, uncovered, for 4 to 5 minutes. Return shrimp to skillet; simmer for 1 minute more. Spoon into serving dish.

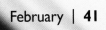

march

ruby martini cactus cooler
cranberry cooler california
lemonade stinging nettle
pomegrnate martini hula
red hot shot ciroc cherry
blossom pineapple pleaser
ruby martini cactus cooler
cranberry cooler california
lemonade stinging nettle
pomegrnate martini hula

HURRICANE

Makes 1 drink

3	ounces passion fruit juice
3	ounces mango juice
2	ounces sweet-and-sour mix
¾	ounce dark rum, *Myers's*®
½	ounce spiced rum, *Captain Morgan® Original Spiced Rum*

In a cocktail shaker, combine passion fruit juice, mango juice, sweet-and-sour mix, dark rum, and spiced rum. Add ice. Cover, shake; serve.

PESTO-STUFFED MUSHROOMS

Prep 25 minutes   **Bake** 20 minutes   **Makes** 24 mushrooms

	No-stick cooking spray, Pam®
24	large fresh mushrooms, 1½ to 2 inches in diameter
¼	cup extra virgin olive oil
1	cup San Francisco sourdough stuffing mix, *Stovetop*®
½	cup boiling water
1	cup ricotta cheese
¾	cup shredded mozzarella cheese, *Sargento*®
¼	cup grated Parmesan cheese, *Sargento*®
2	tablespoons pesto, *Classico*®
2	teaspoons garlic blend, *Gourmet Garden*®

1. Preheat oven to 375 degrees F. Coat a rimmed baking pan with cooking spray; set aside. Wipe mushrooms clean with paper towels; remove stems and discard. Brush inside and outside with olive oil.

2. In a medium bowl, combine stuffing mix and the boiling water. Cover and let stand for 5 minutes or until slightly softened. Stir in ricotta, mozzarella, 2 tablespoons of Parmesan cheese, pesto, and garlic. Spoon stuffing mixture into mushroom caps. Place caps on prepared baking sheet. Sprinkle with remaining 2 tablespoons Parmesan cheese. Bake for 20 to 25 minutes or until golden brown.

RUBY MARTINI

Makes 1 drink

2	ounces pink grapefruit juice
1½	ounces citrus flavored vodka, *Smirnoff*®
¼	ounce orange liqueur, *Grand Marnier*®
¼	ounce sugar syrup
	Ice cubes

In a cocktail shaker, combine grapefruit juice, vodka, orange liqueur, and sugar syrup. Add ice; cover and shake until very cold. Strain into a martini glass.

VODKA SANGRIA

Makes 11 drinks

2	cups ice cubes
1	bottle (750-milliliter) white wine, *Sterling Vineyards*®
6	ounces vodka, *Cîroc*®
3	ounces orange liqueur, *Grand Marnier*®
3	ounces pomegranate juice
3	ounces orange juice
3	ounces lemon juice
2	ounces white grape juice
2	ounces sugar syrup

Combine all ingredients in a large pitcher; stir to combine. Pour into ice-filled glasses. Garnish with citrus slices and fresh raspberries.

CRANBERRY COOLER

Makes 8 servings

4	cups refrigerated red grapefruit juice
2	tablespoons finely chopped fresh mint leaves
2	teaspoons honey
4	fresh grapefruit slices, halved
	Fresh mint sprigs

In bowl, combine the grapefruit juice, mint, and honey. Pour into 13×9-inch glass pan. Freeze for at least 4 hours. When mixture is frozen, use the tines of fork to scrape the mixture into icy flakes. Place back into the freezer for 1 hour. Spoon mixture into chilled glasses or bowls. Garnish with grapefruit and mint sprigs.

POMEGRANATE MARTINI

Makes 1 drink

1	ounce vodka, *Smirnoff No. 21™*
½	ounce orange liqueur, *Grand Marnier®*
1	splash pomegranate juice
1	splash tonic water
	Ice cubes
	Lemon twist

In a cocktail shaker, combine vodka, orange liqueur, pomegranate juice, and tonic water. Add ice; cover and shake until very cold. Strain into a chilled martini glass. Garnish with a lemon twist.

GOAT CHEESE QUESADILLAS

Prep 15 minutes   **Cook** 5 minutes   **Makes** 4 servings

8	ounces soft goat cheese (chèvre), *Silver Goat®*
5	tablespoons guava jelly, *Knott's®*
8	flour tortillas (6-inch), *Mission®*
	No-stick cooking spray, *Pam®*
	Crumbled Cotija cheese (optional)
1	cup lime-and-cilantro salsa, *Pace®*

1. In a small bowl, stir together goat cheese and guava jelly just until combined. Spread cheese mixture on 4 of the tortillas; top with remaining tortillas.

2. Coat an extra-large skillet with cooking spray. Heat skillet over medium-high heat. Add quesadillas. Cook for 5 to 6 minutes or until lightly browned, turning halfway through cooking.

3. Cut quesadillas into wedges. Sprinkle with Cotija cheese (optional). Serve warm with salsa for dipping.

CALIFORNIA LEMONADE

Makes 1 drink

2	ounces orange juice
¾	ounce vodka, *Smirnoff® No.21™*
¼	ounce gin, *Tanqueray®*
¼	ounce cognac
¼	ounce grenadine
1	splash lime juice
1	splash sugar syrup
	Ice cubes
	Half-slices lime or lemon
	Fresh raspberries

In a cocktail shaker, combine orange juice, vodka, gin, cognac, grenadine, lime juice, and sugar syrup. Cover and shake vigorously. Serve in an ice-filled glass. Garnish.

CACTUS COOLER

Makes 1 drink

1½ ounces watermelon flavored vodka, *Smirnoff*®
1 splash melon liqueur
  Ice cubes

In a cocktail shaker, combine vodka and melon liqueur. Add ice; cover and shake until very cold. Strain into chilled shot glasses.

PETITE LIME CHEESECAKES

Prep 10 minutes   **Freeze** 10 minutes   **Makes** 6 mini cheesecakes

1 package (8-ounce) cream cheese softened, *Philadelphia*®
½ cup sugar, *Domino*®/*C&H*®
3 tablespoons lime curd, *Dickinson's*®
1 package (4-ounce) graham cracker crumb tart shells, *Keebler*®
  Frozen whipped topping, thawed, *Cool Whip*®
  Lime slices
  Sugar

1. In a medium mixing bowl, beat cream cheese and ½ cup sugar with an electric mixer on medium speed until creamy. Add lime curd and beat on low speed until just combined.

2. Spoon cream cheese mixture into 6 tart shells. Place tart shells on a small baking sheet and freeze about 10 minutes or until firm. Garnish each with a dollop of whipped topping and a lime slice that has been sprinkled with additional sugar.

STINGING NETTLE

Makes 1 drink

1 ounce Irish whiskey, *Black Bush*®
½ ounce crème de menthe
  Ice cubes
  Peppermint candy, crushed

In a cocktail shaker, combine whiskey and crème de menthe. Add ice; cover and shake until very cold. Strain into a chilled martini glass. Garnish with peppermint candy.

RED HOT SHOT

Makes 1 drink

1	ounce tequila, *Jose Cuervo Especial*®
1	splash tomato juice
	Dash hot pepper sauce, *Tabasco*®
	Ice cold beer, *Red Stripe*®

In a chilled tall glass, combine tequila, tomato juice, and hot pepper sauce. Stir to mix. Serve with ice cold beer as a chaser.

SPICY COCONUT SHRIMP

Start to Finish 15 minutes   **Makes** 4 servings

1	tablespoon canola oil, *Wesson*®
1	teaspoon chopped fresh garlic
1	cup light coconut milk
¼	cup low-sodium chicken broth, *Swanson*®
2	teaspoons low-sodium soy sauce, *Kikkoman*®
¼	cup half-and-half
1	pound cooked, peeled, and deveined medium shrimp with tails
2	tablespoons fresh cilantro leaves

1. In a large skillet, heat oil over medium heat. Add garlic; cook until fragrant. Stir in coconut milk, chicken broth, and soy sauce. Bring to a boil; reduce heat to a simmer. Cook for 5 minutes.

2. Stir in half-and-half; return to a simmer without boiling. Add cooked shrimp and heat through. Garnish with cilantro.

HULA GIRL

Makes 4 drinks

2	cans (12 ounces each) guava nectar
2	cups unsweetened pineapple juice
1	package (16-ounce) frozen strawberries
¼	cup sugar
3	cups crushed ice
	Crushed ice
	Fresh raspberries

In a blender, combine guava nectar, pineapple juice, strawberries, and sugar. Add 3 cups ice. Blend until smooth. Serve over additional ice. Garnish with raspberries.

CÎROC CHERRY BLOSSOM

Makes | drink

- 1¼ **ounces vodka,** *Cîroc*®
- ¾ **ounce pomegranate liqueur**
- ¾ **ounce lemon juice**
- ½ **ounce sugar syrup**
- **Ice cubes**
- 1 **splash Champagne or club soda**
- **Fresh pineapple chunk**

In a cocktail shaker, combine vodka, pomegranate liqueur, lemon juice, and sugar syrup. Add ice; cover and shake until very cold. Strain into a glass. Add additional ice. Add Champagne. Garnish with pineapple.

PINEAPPLE PLEASER

Makes | drink

- **Ice cubes**
- 3 **ounces unsweetened pineapple juice**
- 1½ **ounces tequila,** *Jose Cuervo Especial*®
- 1½ **ounces lemon juice**
- ¾ **ounce grenadine syrup**
- **Club soda**
- **Fresh pineapple wedge**

Fill a tall glass halfway with ice. Add pineapple juice, tequila, lemon juice, and grenadine syrup; stir to combine. Top with club soda. Garnish with pineapple wedge.

april

bahama mama shimmer-tini
buttercream martini berry
encore tropical smoothie
pom margarita peach-mango
smoothie brazilian daiquiri
martini dream watermelon
soda roman column startini
bahama mama shimmer-tini
buttercream martini berry
encore tropical smoothie

SHIMMER-TINI

Makes 1 drink

1½	ounces vanilla flavored vodka, *Smirnoff®*
1½	ounces unsweetened pineapple juice
2	tablespoons cream of coconut
¾	ounce key lime juice
	Ice cubes
	Lime slice

In a cocktail shaker, combine vodka, pineapple juice, cream of coconut, and key lime juice. Add ice; cover and shake until very cold. Strain into a chilled martini glass. Garnish with lime slice.

GREEK LAYERED DIP WITH PITA CHIPS

Start to Finish 20 minutes   **Makes** 10 servings

1	package (14-ounce) pita bread rounds, *Sara Lee®*
	No-stick cooking spray, *Pam®*
4	teaspoons dried Greek seasoning, *Spice Islands®*
1	pound ground lamb
1	teaspoon garlic salt, *Lawry's®*
1	container (16-ounce) prepared hummus, *Athenos®*
1½	cups tzatziki (gyro sauce), *Sahara®*
1	cup shredded iceberg lettuce, *Ready Pac®*
2	medium roma tomatoes, chopped
½	cup diced red onion, *Ready Pac®*
½	cup pitted kalamata olives, chopped, *Mezzetta®*
1	container (4-ounce) crumbled feta cheese, *Athenos®*

1. Preheat oven to 375 degrees F. Line 1 or 2 baking sheets with aluminum foil. Cut each pita round into 8 wedges. Split each wedge in half horizontally and place, split sides up, on prepared baking sheet(s). Coat pita wedges with cooking spray and sprinkle with 2 teaspoons of the Greek seasoning. Bake in preheated oven for 7 to 10 minutes or until golden brown.

2. Meanwhile, in a large skillet, cook ground lamb over medium-high heat until brown. Drain off fat. Stir in garlic salt and the remaining 2 teaspoons Greek seasoning.

3. Spread hummus in the bottom of a shallow 1½-quart serving bowl. Top with lamb mixture, tzatziki, lettuce, tomatoes, red onion, and olives. Sprinkle with feta cheese. Serve dip at room temperature with baked pita wedges.

ROMAN COLUMN

Makes 1 drink

	Ice cubes
2¼	ounces half-and-half
1	ounce sambuca, *Romana Sambuca®*
½	ounce coffee Irish cream liqueur, *Baileys®*
	Whole coffee beans

Fill a cocktail shaker with ice. Add half-and-half, sambuca, and coffee liqueur. Cover and shake vigorously. Strain into an ice-filled glass. Garnish with whole coffee beans.

DARK CHOCOLATE FONDUE

Prep 3 minutes   **Cook** 7 minutes   **Makes** 6 servings

1	cup heavy cream
½	stick unsalted butter
1	package (12-ounce) semisweet chocolate morsels, *Hershey's®*
1	package (12-ounce) milk chocolate morsels, *Hershey's®*
	Dippers: sliced apples, bananas, strawberries, crisp cookies, pretzels, and cubed pound cake, *Sara Lee®*

1. In a large saucepan, over medium heat, combine cream and butter. Bring mixture just to a simmer, stirring constantly. Remove pan from heat.

2. Add semisweet and milk chocolate morsels. Stir until melted and smooth. Cool slightly.

3. Transfer to a fondue pot, chafing dish, or ceramic bowl. Serve with apples, bananas, strawberries, cookies, pretzels, and pound cake.

BAHAMA MAMA

Makes 1 drink

1½	ounces piña colada mixer, *Stirrings®*
1¼	ounces spiced rum, *Captain Morgan® Original Spiced Rum*
¾	ounce chocolate liqueur, *Godiva®*
2	cups ice cubes

In a blender, combine piña colada mixer, rum, chocolate liqueur, and ice. Blend until smooth. Pour into a daiquiri or parfait glass.

PEACH-MANGO SMOOTHIE

Makes 1 drink

- 1   **cup ice cubes**
- 1   **container (6-ounce) fat-free peach yogurt**
- ½   **cup mango nectar**
- ½   **cup frozen mango chunks**
- ½   **cup frozen sliced peaches**
- ¼   **block silken soft tofu, cut into chunks**

In a blender, combine ice, yogurt, mango nectar, the ½ cup mango, the ½ cup peaches, and tofu. Cover and blend for 30 to 60 seconds or until smooth. Garnish with additional mango, peaches, and cherries.

CRAB CUCUMBER ROUNDS

Prep 10 minutes   **Chill** 30 minutes   **Makes** 16 cucumber rounds

- ¼   **cup mayonnaise, *Best Foods®/Hellmann's®***
- 1   **teaspoon prepared horseradish, *Morehouse®***
- ½   **teaspoon Dijon mustard, *French's®***
- ½   **teaspoon Worcestershire sauce, *Lea & Perrins®***
- 1   **can (4.25-ounce) crabmeat, drained, *Geisha®***
- ½   **unpeeled English hothouse cucumber, cut crosswise into ¼-inch slices (16 total)**
-    **Pimiento-stuffed green olives, sliced, *Star®***

1. In a small bowl, combine mayonnaise, horseradish, mustard, and Worcestershire sauce. Gently stir in crabmeat. Cover and chill in refrigerator for 30 minutes.

2. On a serving tray, arrange cucumber slices in a single layer. Spoon about 1 tablespoon crabmeat mixture on each cucumber slice. Garnish each with an olive slice.

TROPICAL SMOOTHIE

Makes 2 drinks

- 1½   **cups ice cubes**
- 1   **small banana, cut into chunks**
- 1   **can (8-ounce) crushed pineapple**
- 1   **container (6-ounce) vanilla yogurt**
- ¾   **cup fat-free milk**
- ½   **cup light coconut milk**
- ⅓   **cup unsweetened pineapple juice**
- 1   **tablespoon packed brown sugar**
-    **Fresh pineapple wedges**

In a blender, combine all ingredients except pineapple wedges. Cover and blend until smooth. Pour into glasses. Garnish with pineapple wedges.

BRAZILIAN DAIQUIRI

Makes 1 drink

3	ounces freshly squeezed lime juice
2	lime wedges
1½	ounces white rum, *Oronoco®*
1	splash limoncello liqueur
1	splash sugar syrup

Fill a cocktail shaker with crushed ice. Add all ingredients. Cover and shake vigorously. Strain into a glass over ice.

APRICOT SHORTCAKES

Start to Finish 20 minutes   **Makes** 6 servings

1	carton (8-ounce) mascarpone cheese, *BelGioioso®*
1	container (8-ounce) frozen extra-creamy whipped dessert topping, thawed, *Cool Whip®*
1	teaspoon shredded lemon zest
½	teaspoon almond extract, *McCormick®*
1	package (5-ounce) individual sponge shortcake cups, *Van de Kamp's®*
1	can (15¼-ounce) unpeeled apricot halves in heavy syrup, *Del Monte®*
2	tablespoons brandy, *Christian Brothers®*
	Slivered almonds, toasted

1. In a large bowl, whisk mascarpone cheese. Stir in half of the whipped topping, lemon zest, extract, and a pinch of *salt*. Fill shortcake cups with cheese mixture.

2. Drain apricots, reserving syrup. Set apricots aside. In a small saucepan, combine the reserved apricot syrup and brandy. Cook until thick. Add apricots. Spoon apricot mixture over shortcake cups. Top with the remaining whipped topping. Garnish with almonds.

BUTTERCREAM MARTINI

Makes 1 drink

1 ½   **ounces half-and-half or light cream**

1   **ounce spiced rum,** *Captain Morgan®*
        Original Spiced Rum

½   **ounce butterscotch schnapps**

½   **ounce vanilla schnapps**

        Ice cubes

        Candy confetti

In a cocktail shaker, combine half-and-half, rum, buttersotch schnapps, and vanilla schnapps. Add ice; cover and shake until very cold. Strain into a chilled martini glass. Garnish with candy confetti.

STARTINI DREAM

Makes I drink

	Ice cubes
I	ounce black cherry flavored vodka, *Smirnoff*®
½	ounce orange liqueur, *Grand Marnier*®
I	splash sweetened lime juice
	Blueberry swizzle sticks

Fill a cocktail shaker with ice. Add all ingredients except swizzle sticks. Cover and shake. Strain into a glass. Garnish with swizzle sticks.

WHITE PIZZA

Prep 15 minutes   **Bake** 15 minutes   **Makes** 4 servings

	No-stick cooking spray, *Pam*®
I	package (13.8-ounce) refrigerated pizza dough, *Pillsbury*®
½	cup roasted garlic Alfredo pasta sauce, *Classico*®
2	cups shredded Italian 5-cheese blend, *Kraft*®
¼	onion, chopped
4	roasted cloves garlic, *Christopher Ranch*®
I	package (6-ounce) refrigerated grilled chicken breast strips, *Louis Rich*®
¼	cup shredded Parmesan cheese, *Kraft*®
I	teaspoon dried Italian seasoning, *McCormick*®
	Fresh rosemary sprigs

1. Preheat oven to 425 degrees F. Coat a baking sheet with cooking spray. Unroll pizza dough onto sheet. Press dough into a 13×9-inch rectangle.

2. Bake about 7 minutes or until crust is lightly browned. Spread Alfredo sauce over crust, leaving a 1-inch border. Sprinkle with Italian cheese, onion, and garlic. Arrange chicken on pizza. Sprinkle with Parmesan and Italian seasoning. Bake 8 to 10 minutes more or until crust is golden and cheese is melted. Garnish with rosemary.

BERRY ENCORE

Makes I drink

I	ounce blueberry flavored vodka, *Smirnoff*®
½	ounce orange liqueur, *Grand Marnier*®
I	splash sweetened lime juice
	Ice cubes
	Fresh blueberries

In a cocktail shaker, combine vodka, orange liqueur, and lime juice. Add ice; cover and shake until very cold. Strain into a chilled glass. Garnish with fresh blueberries.

WATERMELON SODA

Makes 6 servings

1	cup watermelon flavored vodka, *Smirnoff*®
1	12-ounce can frozen lemonade concentrate
2	tablespoons packaged lemon gelatin mix
1	tablespoon granulated sugar

In a blender, combine vodka, lemonade concentrate, gelatin, and sugar. Cover and pulse to mix. Add ice to almost fill blender. Cover and continue to pulse until ice is crushed. Pour into glasses over ice and serve.

SWEET PEPPER POPPERS

Prep 25 minutes   **Bake** 20 minutes   **Makes** about 50 poppers

	No-stick cooking spray, *Pam*®
2	pints baby red, yellow, and orange bell peppers and/or jalapeño chile peppers
1	package (8-ounce) cream cheese, softened, *Philadelphia*®
1	cup shredded pepper-Jack cheese (4 ounces), *Tillamook*®
2	green onions, finely chopped
1	cup fresh chunky salsa

1. Preheat oven to 300 degrees F. Lightly coat a baking sheet with cooking spray. Set aside.

2. Cut each pepper lengthwise through stem. Using a spoon, scrape out seeds and veins. Set aside. In a medium bowl, stir together cream cheese, shredded cheese, and green onions. Fill hollowed-out peppers with cheese mixture. Place peppers on a baking sheet. Bake for 20 to 25 minutes or until heated through.

3. Top each pepper with a spoonful of the fresh salsa.

POM MARGARITA MARTINI

Makes 1 drink

    Ice cubes
3   **ounces lime margarita drink mix,** *Jose Cuervo*®
2   **ounces pomegranate juice**
1½ **ounces tequila,** *Jose Cuervo Especial*®
    Salt (optional)
    Lime or lemon slice

Fill a cocktail shaker half full of ice. Add margarita mix, pomegranate juice, and tequila. Wet the rim of a chilled martini glass with *water* and dip rim in salt. Cover and shake tequila mixture vigorously. Carefully strain into martini glass. Garnish with lime or lemon slice.

may

café roma martini coconut
colada champagne cosmo
kiwi kooler cucumber sake
shots chocolate berry diva
creamsicle martini river run
cocktail don's delight kiwi
kooler strawberry swirl
watermelon fizz strawberry
slide passionpolitan café
roma martini creamsicle

CAFÉ ROMA MARTINI

Makes 1 drink

- 1½ ounces half-and-half
- 1 ounce sambuca, *Romana Sambuca*®
- 1 ounce Irish cream liqueur, *Baileys*®

In a cocktail shaker, combine all ingredients with *ice cubes*; cover and shake until very cold. Strain into a chilled martini glass. Garnish with coffee beans.

CHERRY CRUMBLE

Prep 15 minutes **Cook** 2 hours (High)
Bake 12 minutes **Makes** 8 servings

FOR SLOW-COOKED CHERRIES

- 1 bag (16-ounce) frozen cherries, *C&W*®
- 1 cup sugar, *Domino*®/*C&H*®
- ½ cup dried cherries, *Maiani*®
- ¼ cup cherry brandy
- 2 tablespoons quick-cooking tapioca, *Minute*®

FOR CRUMBLE TOPPING

- ¾ cup low-fat granola, *Quaker*® *100% Natural*
- ½ cup packaged biscuit mix, *Bisquick*®
- 10 gingersnaps, crushed, *Nabisco*®
- 2 tablespoons butter, melted

1. For Slow-Cooked Cherries: In a 4-quart slow cooker, combine all ingredients and ¾ cup of *water*. Cover and cook on High heat setting for 2 to 4 hours.

2. Preheat oven to 350 degrees F 30 minutes before Slow-Cooked Cherries are ready. Line a baking sheet with aluminum foil; set aside.

3. For Crumble Topping: In a bowl, stir together granola, biscuit mix, gingersnaps, and butter. Spread on baking sheet. Bake 12 minutes. Spoon cherries into dessert dishes. Sprinkle with topping.

COCONUT COLADA

Makes 1 drink

¼	**cup honey**
¼	**cup coconut flakes, toasted**
	Ice cubes
2	**ounces pineapple-coconut juice**
1	**splash sweetened lime juice**
1	**ounce vanilla flavored vodka,** *Smirnoff®*
½	**ounce half-and-half**
½	**ounce banana schnapps**
	Lime slice

Pour honey onto a plate. Place coconut on another plate. Dip the rim of a chilled glass into honey; dip in coconut. Fill cocktail shaker with ice. Add pineapple-coconut juice, lime juice, vodka, half-and-half, and banana schnapps. Cover and shake vigorously. Carefully strain into glass. Garnish with lime slice.

CHAMPAGNE COSMO

Makes 7 drinks

1	bottle (750-milliliter) white wine, *Sterling Vineyards® Chardonnay*
3	cups lemon-lime soda
1	can (12-ounce) frozen pink lemonade concentrate, thawed
½	cup citrus vodka, *Ketel One Citroen®*
	Lemon slices

In a large pitcher, combine wine, soda, lemonade concentrate, and vodka. Chill in refrigerator for 1 hour. Pour into 6 chilled glasses. Garnish each with a lemon slice.

CUCUMBER-RED PEPPER RAITA

Prep 20 minutes   **Bake** 10 minutes   **Chill** 1 hour   **Makes** 6 servings

FOR NAAN-STYLE FLATBREAD

	No-stick cooking spray, *Pam®*
1	package (13.8-ounce) refrigerated pizza crust, *Pillsbury®*
2	tablespoons butter, melted
½	teaspoon cumin seeds, *McCormick®*
½	teaspoon poppy seeds, *McCormick®*
½	teaspoon sesame seeds, *McCormick®*

FOR CUCUMBER-RED PEPPER RAITA

1	English hothouse cucumber, peeled and finely chopped
½	red bell pepper, cored, seeded, and finely chopped
½	cup plain yogurt, *Dannon®*
2	tablespoons finely chopped fresh mint
1	jalapeño chile pepper, finely chopped

1. Preheat oven to 400 degrees F. Lightly coat a baking sheet with cooking spray; set aside.

2. For Flatbread: Unroll pizza crust onto prepared baking sheet. Press dough to ¼-inch thickness; brush with melted butter. Sprinkle dough with cumin seeds, poppy seeds, and sesame seeds. Bake for 10 to 12 minutes or until light golden brown. Remove from oven and cut into 6 pieces.

3. For Raita: In a medium bowl, combine cucumber, bell pepper, yogurt, mint, and jalapeño pepper. Cover and chill in refrigerator for at least 1 hour. Serve with flatbread.

KIWI KOOLER

Makes 2 drinks

4	kiwifruits, peeled and chopped
I	cup guava nectar
I	carton (6-ounce) vanilla fat-free yogurt
3	ounces spiced rum, *Captain Morgan® Original Spiced Rum*
I	tablespoon frozen limeade concentrate
I	tablespoon chopped fresh mint
I	cup ice cubes

In a blender, combine all ingredients. Cover and blend on high about 40 seconds or until smooth. Pour into chilled glasses.

STUFFED CUCUMBERS

Prep 25 minutes   **Makes** 16 cucumber cups

2	unpeeled English hothouse cucumbers
I	container (8-ounce) cream cheese, softened, *Philadelphia®*
I	container (8-ounce) sour cream, *Knudsen®*
I	package (3-ounce) lox or smoked salmon, chopped into small pieces
I	shallot, finely chopped
2	tablespoons lemon juice, *ReaLemon®*
	Dill sprigs

1. Cut off ends of cucumbers. Create stripes on cucumbers with a zester or vegetable peeler. Cut each cucumber into 1½- to 2-inch pieces. Carefully scoop out seeds and flesh from top two-thirds of each round.

2. For filling, combine cream cheese and sour cream. Stir in salmon, shallot, lemon juice, and a pinch of *salt* and *pepper*. Transfer filling to a pastry bag fitted with a large star tip. Pipe filling into cucumber cups. Garnish with dill.

CUCUMBER SAKE SHOTS

Makes 4 drinks

1	unpeeled English hothouse cucumber
¾	ounce lime juice
1	tablespoon sugar
4	ounces spiced rum, *Captain Morgan® Silver Spiced Rum*
1	ounce sake
	Ice cubes

For cucumber shot glasses, cut off ends of cucumber. Create stripes on outside of cucumber by using a zester or vegetable peeler to peel length of cucumber, leaving every other section intact. Cut cucumber into four 2-inch pieces. With a melon baller or using tip of a small spoon, scoop out seeds and cucumber flesh from center of each piece, being careful not to cut through the other side and leaving a ½-inch bottom. Set aside.

For drink, in a blender, combine cucumber flesh with lime juice. Cover and blend about 15 seconds or until smooth. Pour cucumber puree through a fine-mesh strainer, reserving ½ cup cucumber juice. Stir in sugar.

In a cocktail shaker, combine reserved cucumber juice, rum, and sake. Add ice; cover and shake until very cold. Strain into cucumber shot glasses. Serve immediately.

CHOCOLATE BERRY DIVA

Makes 1 drink

4	ounces club soda
1	ounce chocolate liqueur, *Godiva®*
1	ounce raspberry liqueur
	Ice cubes, cranberries

In a glass, combine soda, chocolate liqueur, and raspberry liqueur. Add ice. Garnish with cranberries.

ASIAGO-HAM PINWHEELS

Prep 20 minutes   **Bake** 15 minutes   **Makes** 16 pinwheels

1	frozen puff pastry sheet, thawed according to package directions, *Pepperidge Farm®*
2	tablespoons apricot preserves, *Smucker's®*
1½	tablespoons Dijon mustard, *Grey Poupon®*
¼	cup dried currants, *Sun-Maid®*
¼	cup shredded Asiago cheese, *DiGiorno®*
1	package (6-ounce) thinly sliced cooked ham, *Hillshire Farm®*

1. Preheat oven to 400 degrees F. Line 2 baking sheets with parchment paper. On a lightly floured surface, unfold puff pastry sheet. Using a rolling pin, roll sheet into a 14×11-inch rectangle.

2. In a bowl, combine preserves and mustard. Spread mixture over puff pastry, leaving a ½-inch border. Sprinkle with currants and cheese. Top with ham slices. Starting with a short side, roll rectangle up in a spiral. Using a pastry brush, lightly moisten edge with *water*; pinch to seal seam. Slice pastry roll into sixteen ½-inch slices. Place pinwheels, cut sides down, on prepared baking sheets. Bake for 15 minutes or until puffed and golden brown. Serve warm.

CREAMSICLE MARTINI

Makes 1 drink

1	ounce vanilla flavored vodka, *Smirnoff*®
½	ounce strawberry nectar
½	ounce strawberry liqueur
1½	ounces half-and-half
	Fresh strawberry, sliced (optional)

Fill a cocktail shaker with ice. Add vodka, nectar, liqueur, and half-and-half. Cover and shake vigorously. Strain into a chilled martini glass. Garnish with a sliced strawberry (optional).

DON'S DELIGHT

Makes 1 drink

1	ounce unsweetened pineapple juice
¾	ounce tequila, *Don Julio® Blanco*
¾	ounce melon liqueur
	Ice cubes
	Kiwifruit slice
	Frozen whipped dessert topping, thawed
	Toasted macadamia nuts, chopped

In a glass, combine pineapple juice, tequila, and melon liqueur. Add ice and kiwifruit slice. Top with whipped topping and sprinkle with macadamia nuts.

CLUB 55 HARICOTS VERTS

Makes 4 servings   **Prep** 10 minutes   **Microwave** 5 minutes

2	packages (8 ounces each) ready-to-cook haricots verts French beans, *Greenline®*
½	cup water
2	tablespoons sour cream, *Knudsen®*
1	teaspoon lemon juice, *ReaLemon®*
	Salt and freshly ground black pepper
¼	cup shaved Parmesan cheese

1. In a large microwave-safe bowl, combine beans and water. Microwave, covered, for 5 to 7 minutes on high-heat setting (100 percent power) or just until tender. Drain.

2. Add sour cream and lemon juice to beans. Toss to coat. Season to taste with salt and pepper. Garnish with Parmesan cheese.

RIVER RUN COCKTAIL

Makes 1 drink

3	fresh mint leaves
	Crushed ice
½	lime
1	bottle (12-ounce) beer, *Red Stripe®*
	Fresh mint sprig

Place the 3 mint leaves in bottom of a glass. Fill with crushed ice. Squeeze lime juice into glass. Pour in beer. Garnish with mint sprig.

STRAWBERRY SWIRL

Makes 1 drink

½   cup ice cubes
1½   ounces strawberry flavored vodka, *Smirnoff®*
½   cup fresh whole strawberries
    Fresh whole strawberry

In a blender, combine ice and vodka. Add the ½ cup strawberries. Cover and blend until smooth. Pour into chilled glass. Garnish with additional strawberry.

STRAWBERRY PARFAIT

Start to Finish 10 minutes   **Makes** 4 servings

1   can (15-ounce) strawberry pie filling, *Comstock More Fruit®*
⅓   cup candied walnuts, chopped, *Emerald®*
½   teaspoon ground allspice, *McCormick®*
8   oatmeal cookies, *Mother's®*
    Caramel sauce, *Mrs. Richardson's®*
1   pint vanilla ice cream, *Häagen Dazs®*
4   whole strawberries

1. In a medium bowl, combine strawberry pie filling, walnuts, and allspice. Set aside. Crumble 2 of the oatmeal cookies into the bottom of each of 4 parfait glasses. Drizzle each with caramel sauce. Divide strawberry mixture among glasses. Top with a scoop of ice cream. Garnish with strawberries.

WATERMELON FIZZ

Makes 2 drinks

2	cups seedless watermelon chunks
6	ounces club soda
2	tablespoons frozen limeade concentrate
1	tablespoon chopped fresh mint
10	ice cubes
3	ounces watermelon flavored vodka, *Smirnoff*®
1	tablespoon sugar
	Whole strawberries

In a blender, combine watermelon, club soda, limeade concentrate, fresh mint, ice, vodka, and sugar. Cover and blend until smooth. Pour into chilled glasses. Garnish with strawberries.

PASSIONPOLITAN

Makes 10 drinks

2	cups pineapple juice
2	cups cranberry juice
½	cup tequila, *Don Julio® Blanco*
½	cup vodka, *Cîroc®*
½	cup passion fruit rum, *Captain Morgan Parrot Bay® Passion Fruit*
½	cup gin, *Tanqueray®*

In a pitcher of *ice*, combine all ingredients. Stir and serve over ice.

ORIENTAL PORK PURSES

Prep 25 minutes   **Cook** 8 minutes per batch   **Makes** 24 purses

1	package (12-ounce) pork sausage, *Johnsonville®*
2	green onions, minced
1	tablespoon soy sauce, *Kikkoman®*
1	tablespoon hoisin sauce, *Sun Luck®*
½	teaspoon dried minced garlic, *McCormick®*
24	wonton wrappers, *Dynasty®*
	No-stick cooking spray, *Pam®*
	Chili garlic sauce

1. For filling, combine sausage, green onions, soy sauce, hoisin sauce, and garlic. Lay out 8 wonton wrappers on a clean surface and brush edges with *water*. Place 1 tablespoon pork mixture into center of each wrapper. Gather edges together over filling. Press edges together, enclosing filling. Repeat. Cover purses with a kitchen towel.

2. In a large pot, place a metal steamer rack. Fill pot with ½ inch of water, making sure rack does not touch water. Coat rack with cooking spray. Bring water to a simmer. Working in batches, arrange purses 1 inch apart. Cover and steam 8 minutes or until internal temperature reaches 160 degrees F. Serve with chili garlic sauce.

STRAWBERRY SLIDE

Makes 1 drink

1¼	ounces white rum, *Oronoco®*
1½	ounces pomegranate juice
¼	ounce orange liqueur, *Grand Marnier®*
	Whipped topping, thawed

Combine rum, pomegranate juice, and orange liqueur in an ice-filled cocktail shaker. Shake and strain into a chilled martini glass. Top with whipped topping.

cuervo caribbean mist
cosmorita california lemon
lemon cream martini white
wine cooler daffodil driver
tea-tini watermelon splash
shimmering shiver banana
colada pineapple cooler
lemon teaser daffodil driver
cuervo caribbean mist
cosmorita california lemon
lemon cream martini white

CUERVO CARIBBEAN MIST

Makes 1 drink

    Ice cubes
1½ **ounces unsweetened pineapple juice**
1½ **ounces orange juice**
1 **ounce tequila,** *Jose Cuervo Especial®*
½ **ounce blue curacao**
    Orange slice

Fill a glass halfway with ice. Add pineapple juice, orange juice, tequila, and blue curacao; stir to combine. Garnish with orange slice.

HULA HULA PORK KABOBS

Prep 20 minutes   **Marinate** 2 to 24 hours
Grill 8 minutes   **Makes** 6 servings

1¼ **pounds pork tenderloin, trimmed**
¼ **cup sesame-ginger marinade,** *Lawry's®*
¼ **cup chili sauce,** *Heinz®*
¼ **cup soy sauce,** *Kikkoman®*
¼ **cup dry sherry,** *Christian Brothers®*
1 **cup fresh pineapple wedges, cut into 1-inch chunks,** *Ready Pac®*
1 **green bell pepper, cut into 1-inch squares**
    Green onion curls

1. Cut pork into 1-inch cubes. Place pork cubes in a large zip-top plastic bag. For marinade, in a small bowl, combine sesame-ginger marinade, chili sauce, soy sauce, and sherry. Reserve ½ cup of the sesame-ginger mixture for basting. Pour the remaining mixture into bag. Squeeze out air and seal. Gently massage to combine ingredients. Marinate in refrigerator for 2 hours or overnight.

2. Meanwhile, soak 10-inch wooden skewers in water for 1 hour.

3. Remove pork from the marinade; discard marinade. Drain skewers. Alternately thread pork, pineapple, and green pepper onto skewers.

4. Set up grill for direct cooking over medium-high heat. When ready to start cooking, brush grill with *oil*. Place skewers on hot oiled grill. Cook for 8 to 12 minutes or until pork is cooked through, turning occasionally and basting with reserved sesame-ginger mixture for the first half of cooking. Discard remaining basting mixture. Serve kabobs hot. Garnish with green onion curls.

CARAMELIZED ONIONS AND APPLES WITH BRIE

Prep 45 minutes   **Cook** 12 hours (Low)   **Makes** 12 servings

2	packages (14 ounces each) sliced green apples, *Chiquita*®
2	large sweet onions, sliced into thick rounds
½	cup golden raisins, *Sun-Maid*®
⅓	cup packed light brown sugar, *Domino*®/*C&H*®
1	packet (1.8-ounce) white sauce mix, *Knorr*®
1	tablespoon fines herbes, *Spice Islands*®
1	stick (½ cup) butter, cut into small pieces
	No-stick cooking spray, *Pam*®
½	package (17.3-ounce) frozen puff pastry (1 sheet), thawed, *Pepperidge Farm*®
1	wheel (13.2-ounce) baby Brie, *Alouette*®

1. In a large bowl, combine apples, onions, raisins, brown sugar, white sauce mix, and fines herbes; toss well. Place mixture in a 5-quart slow cooker; dot with butter. Cover and cook on Low heat setting for 12 hours.

2. Forty minutes before serving, preheat oven to 400 degrees F. Coat a baking sheet with no-stick cooking spray; set aside.

3. Unroll pastry sheet. Place Brie wheel in the center of the puff pastry and wrap cheese by bringing ends of pastry together toward the center of the wheel. Carefully turn cheese over, folding pastry ends securely under wheel. Lay on prepared baking sheet, folded side down. Bake for 25 minutes or until light golden brown. Let cool 10 minutes.

4. Serve pastry-wrapped Brie warm with caramelized onion and apple mixture.

CALIFORNIA LEMON

Makes 1 drink

1¼	ounces gin, *Tanqueray*®
1	ounce lemon drop cocktail mixer, *Stirrings*®
¼	ounce blood orange bitters, *Stirrings*®
	Ice cubes
1	lemon wedge

In a cocktail shaker, combine gin, lemon drop mixer, and blood orange bitters. Add ice; cover and shake until very cold. Strain into a chilled glass. Garnish with lemon wedge.

LEMON CREAM MARTINI

Makes 1 drink

	Lemon-flavor drink rimmer, *Stirrings*®
1	ounce vanilla flavored vodka, *Smirnoff*®
½	ounce lemon liqueur
	Ice cubes
1	splash lemon-lime soda

Wet the rim of a chilled martini glass with *water*. Dip the rim in lemon-flavor drink rimmer. In a cocktail shaker, combine vodka and lemon liqueur. Add ice; cover and shake until very cold. Strain into prepared glass. Add lemon-lime soda.

WHITE WINE COOLER

Makes 6 drinks

1	**bottle (750 milliliter) white wine such as Riesling, chilled,** *Trimbach*®
1	**can (15-ounce) sliced peaches in heavy syrup**
½	**cup orange liqueur,** *Grand Marnier*®
½	**cup orange juice**
¼	**cup sugar**
1	**orange, sliced**

In a large pitcher, combine wine, peaches with syrup, orange liqueur, orange juice, and sugar. Stir well. Add orange slices to pitcher. Cover and chill for 1 hour. Pour into 6 wineglasses. Serve immediately.

CHILI QUESADILLAS

Prep 10 minutes   **Cook** 12 minutes   **Makes** 8 servings

2	**tablespoons canola oil**
4	**flour or corn tortilla wraps (10-inch),** *Mission*®
½	**cup shredded Monterey Jack cheese**
1	**cup canned chili with beans,** *Hormel*®
¼	**cup sour cream**

1. In a large skillet, heat 1 tablespoon canola oil over medium-high heat. Place 1 tortilla in skillet. Sprinkle with 2 tablespoons cheese. Top with half of the chili and another 2 tablespoons of the cheese.

2. Put a second tortilla on top. Cook about 6 minutes or until tortillas are slightly browned and cheese is melted, turning once halfway through cooking. Repeat with remaining ingredients. Cut into wedges. Serve with sour cream.

COSMORITA

Makes 1 drink

- **Ice cubes**
- **3   ounces cranberry juice**
- **1½ ounces tequila, *Jose Cuervo Especial*®**
- **1   splash sweetened lime juice**
- **Salt**
- **Lime slice**

Fill a cocktail shaker with ice. Add cranberry juice, tequila, and lime juice. Cover and shake vigorously. Wet the rim of a chilled martini glass with *water*. Dip the rim in salt. Carefully strain cranberry juice mixture into martini glass. Garnish with a lime slice.

DAFFODIL DRIVER

Makes 1 drink

1	ounce tequila, *Jose Cuervo Especial*®
¼	ounce apricot brandy
¼	ounce orange liqueur, *Grand Marnier*®
	Ice cubes, apricot nectar
	Orange slice, lemon slice

In a cocktail shaker, combine tequila, brandy, and liqueur. Add ice. Cover and shake until very cold. Strain into a glass filled with ice. Top with apricot nectar. Garnish with orange and lemon slice.

TUSCAN MEATBALLS WITH MARINARA SAUCE

Prep 20 minutes   **Soak** 1 hour   **Grill** 12 minutes   **Makes** 6 servings

FOR TUSCAN TURKEY MEATBALL KABOBS

1¼	pounds uncooked ground turkey
1	jar (2-ounce) diced pimiento, drained, *Dromedary*®
2	tablespoons balsamic vinaigrette, *Newman's Own*®
1	envelope (1.3-ounce) parma rosa sauce mix, *Knorr*®
1	tablespoon dried Italian seasoning, *McCormick*®
1	teaspoon bottled crushed garlic, *Gourmet Garden*®
1	red bell pepper, cut into 1-inch squares
1	green bell pepper, cut into 1-inch squares
½	red onion, cut into 1-inch squares

FOR MARINARA DIPPING SAUCE

1	cup marinara sauce, *Barilla*®
2	tablespoons balsamic vinaigrette, *Newman's Own*®
2	teaspoons dried Italian seasoning, *McCormick*®
½	teaspoon bottled crushed garlic, *Gourmet Garden*®

1. Soak 12-inch wooden skewers in water for 1 hour. For Tuscan Turkey Meatball Kabobs: In a bowl, combine ground turkey, pimiento, balsamic vinaigrette, sauce mix, Italian seasoning, and garlic. Form mixture into 1-inch meatballs. Thread meatballs, peppers, and onion onto skewers. Set up grill for direct cooking over medium heat. When ready to start cooking, brush grate with *oil*. Place skewers on grill. Cook for 12 minutes or until meatballs are cooked through (165 degrees F), turning frequently.

2. For Marinara Dipping Sauce: In a saucepan, stir together marinara sauce, vinaigrette, Italian seasoning, and garlic. Bring to a boil; reduce heat. Simmer 10 minutes. Serve kabobs with sauce.

TEA-TINI

Makes 6 drinks

1	bottle (20-ounce) green tea, chilled
2	cups frozen mixed berries
9	ounces tequila, *Don Julio® Blanco*
2	tablespoons fresh mint leaves
2	cups mixed-berry sparkling water, chilled

In a 2-quart pitcher, combine green tea, frozen berries, tequila, and mint. Add sparkling water; stir gently.

SALMON AVOCADO STACKS

Start to Finish 25 minutes　　**Makes** 4 servings

1	package (8-ounce) thinly sliced smoked salmon (lox-style)
	Kosher salt and freshly ground black pepper
	Champagne vinaigrette, *Girard's®*
1	cup croutons
3	ripe avocados
½	lemon
1	pinch prepared wasabi, *S&B®*
	Fresh chives, cut up

1. Place a 3-inch ring mold on a serving plate. Layer 2 to 3 pieces of the salmon in mold. Season salmon with salt and pepper. Sprinkle a few dashes of vinaigrette over salmon and top with 2 tablespoons of the croutons.

2. Seed, peel, and thinly slice avocados. Place avocado slices in a small bowl. Squeeze lemon juice over avocado slices to prevent discoloration. Add wasabi; toss gently to combine. Place 3 to 4 slices of the avocado on top of croutons. Repeat each layer. Remove ring mold. Repeat to make a total of 4 stacks. Garnish with chives.

WATERMELON SPLASH

Makes 1 drink

- 3   ounces lemon-lime soda
- 1½ ounces watermelon flavored vodka, *Smirnoff*®
- 1   splash cranberry juice
-    Ice cubes

In a chilled glass, combine lemon-lime soda, vodka, and cranberry juice. Add ice. Stir to combine.

SHIMMERING SHIVER

Makes 2 drinks

3½	ounces Irish cream liqueur, *Baileys*®
3½	ounces coffee liqueur

In a blender, combine Irish cream and coffee liquer with ½ cup of ice cubes. Cover and blend until smooth. Pour into a glass.

CRISPY RINGS

Prep 25 minutes   **Cook** 2 minutes per batch   **Makes** 4 servings

3	medium yellow onions, peeled and sliced into ¼-inch rings
½	cup buttermilk
	Canola oil, *Wesson*®
½	cup all-purpose flour, *Pillsbury*®
½	cup cornmeal
1	teaspoon salt
1	teaspoon ground black pepper
1	teaspoon paprika, *McCormick*®

1. In a large bowl, combine onions and buttermilk. Let soak for 5 minutes. In a large saucepan, heat 1½ inches canola oil over medium to medium-high heat until temperature reaches 375 degrees F.

2. In a shallow bowl, combine flour, cornmeal, 1 teaspoon salt, 1 teaspoon pepper, and paprika. Drain onion rings. Working in batches, add a few onion rings to flour mixture and coat evenly.

3. Fry onion rings, a few at a time, for 2 to 3 minutes or until golden brown. Remove onion rings using a slotted spoon or wire strainer. Drain on paper towels. Keep warm in a 300 degrees F oven while cooking remaining onion rings. Sprinkle with additional *salt* and *pepper*. Serve hot.

BANANA COLADA

Makes 1 drink

2   bananas

2   ounces Irish cream liqueur, *Baileys®*

1   ounce coconut rum, *Captain Morgan Parrot Bay® Coconut*

4   ice cubes

In a blender, combine bananas, Irish cream liqueur, rum, and ice. Cover and blend until smooth. Pour into a tall glass. Serve with a straw.

PINEAPPLE COOLER

Makes 1 drink

2	cups ice cubes
1¼	ounces gin, *Tanqueray®*
1	ounce mojito cocktail mixer, *Stirrings®*
½	ounce piña colada cocktail mixer, *Stirrings®*
	Pineapple wedge

In a blender, combine ice, gin, and cocktail mixers. Cover and blend until smooth. Pour into a glass. Garnish with a pineapple wedge.

LEMON TEASER

Makes 1 drink

1¼	ounces vodka, *Smirnoff No. 21*™
½	ounce unsweetened pineapple juice
¼	ounce coconut rum, *Captain Morgan Parrot Bay®* Coconut
¼	ounce orange juice
	Ice cubes
	Orange slice

In a cocktail shaker, combine vodka, pineapple juice, rum, and orange juice. Add ice; cover and shake until very cold. Strain into a glass with additional ice cubes. Garnish with orange slice.

july

blueberry sangria capri fizz
white russian watermelon
spritzer sparkling sangria
sunburst cooler kissable
cranberry margarita citrus
soother mango beach cocktail
blueberry san capri fizz
white russian watermelon
spritzer sparkling sangria
sunburst cooler kissable

BLUEBERRY SANGRIA

Makes 8 drinks

1	bottle (750-milliliter) white wine, *Sterling Vineyards® Chardonnay*
3	cups lemon-lime soda
1½	cups frozen blueberries
1	can (12-ounce) pink lemonade frozen concentrate, thawed
½	cup cognac, *Hennessy®*
	Ice cubes

In a large pitcher, combine wine, soda, blueberries, lemonade concentrate, and cognac. Chill in refrigerator for 1 hour. Pour into tall glasses. Add ice.

WATERMELON SPRITZER

Makes 4 drinks

4	cups watermelon, cut in chunks, seeds removed
2	tablespoons sugar
2	tablespoons lime juice
2	cups sparkling water, chilled

In a blender, combine watermelon, sugar, and lime juice. Cover and process until smooth. Strain into a pitcher. Top with sparkling water. Pour into glasses and serve.

SUNBURST COOLER

Makes 1 drink

- 1   ounce whisky, *George Dickel*®
- 2   tablespoons frozen lemonade concentrate
        Ice cubes
- 1   cup lemon-lime soda
        Maraschino cherry

In a glass, combine whiskey and lemonade concentrate. Add ice; top with lemon-lime soda. Garnish with maraschino cherry.

VEGETABLE QUESADILLAS

Prep 15 minutes   **Grill** 12 minutes   **Makes** 8 servings

- 1   medium zucchini, sliced lengthwise
- 1   medium yellow summer squash, sliced lengthwise
- 1   red bell pepper, cut into strips
- 1   medium sweet onion, sliced
- 1   tablespoon extra virgin olive oil, *Bertolli*®
- ½   teaspoon dried Mexican seasoning, *McCormick*®
- 8   flour tortillas (8-inch), *Mission*®
- 5   ounces soft goat cheese (chèvre), *Silver Goat*®
- ½   cup shredded Monterey Jack cheese, *Sargento*®
        Thick and chunky salsa, *Ortega*®

1. In a large bowl, combine zucchini, yellow squash, red pepper, onion, olive oil, and Mexican seasoning.

2. Set up grill for direct cooking over medium heat. When ready to start cooking, brush grate with *oil*. Place vegetables on hot oiled grill. Cook for 6 to 8 minutes or just until vegetables are tender and lightly browned, turning halfway through grilling. Remove from grill.

3. Spread 4 of the tortillas with goat cheese. Divide grilled vegetables among the cheese-coated tortillas. Top with Monterey Jack cheese and the remaining tortillas. Return to hot oiled grill. Cook for 6 to 8 minutes more or until quesadillas are golden brown and cheese is melted, turning halfway through grilling. Cut quesadillas into wedges. Serve hot with salsa.

SPARKLING SANGRIA

Makes 1 drink

- 1½ ounces sangria cocktail mixer, *Stirrings®*
- 5 ounces extra-dry Champagne

In a chilled flute, combine mixer and Champagne. Garnish.

CAPRI FIZZ

Makes 1 drink

- 2 ounces strawberry nectar
- 1 ounce bitter Italian apéritif
- 1 ounce strawberry flavored vodka, *Smirnoff®*
  Ice cubes, club soda, orange twist

In a glass, combine nectar, apéritif, and vodka. Add ice. Add club soda to fill glass. Garnish with orange twist.

GRILLED JALAPEÑO POPPERS

Prep 20 minutes   **Grill** 6 minutes   **Makes** 12 poppers

- 12 large jalapeño chile peppers
- 1 cup Mexican shredded cheese blend, *Kraft®*
- 6 slices packaged ready-to-serve cooked bacon, crisped in microwave, *Oscar Mayer®*

1. Cut a slit lengthwise down one side of each pepper to create a pocket, being careful to not cut through jalapeño. Leave stem intact and remove seeds and veins. Fill each pepper with cheese. Cut bacon in half crosswise. Wrap each pepper with half-piece of bacon. Secure with a toothpick.

2. Set up grill for direct cooking over medium-high heat. When ready to start cooking, brush grate with *oil*. Place peppers on hot oiled grill and cook for 6 to 10 minutes or until heated through, turning halfway through cooking. Remove from grill. Serve hot.

KISSABLE

Makes 1 drink

- 1½ ounces milk
- ¾ ounce orange flavored vodka, *Smirnoff®*
- ¾ ounce white crème de cacao
- Ice cubes

In a cocktail shaker, combine milk, vodka, and crème de cacao. Add ice; cover and shake until very cold. Strain into a chilled martini glass.

LAMB KEFTA SKEWERS

Prep 25 minutes   **Grill** 12 minutes   **Makes** 16 meatballs

- 8 fresh rosemary stalks (8 to 10 inches)
- 1½ pounds ground lamb
- ¼ cup chopped fresh flat-leaf parsley
- 2 teaspoons chopped fresh rosemary
- 1 teaspoon garlic salt, *Lawry's®*
- 1 teaspoon garam masala, *The Spice Hunter®*
- ½ teaspoon ground black pepper, *McCormick®*
- 24 garlic-stuffed green olives, *Santa Barbara®*
- 4 pita bread rounds, *Sara Lee®*
- Purchased tzatziki sauce

1. Set up grill for direct cooking over medium-high heat. Strip all but the top 1 inch of leaves from rosemary stalks. Wrap tops in foil.

2. In a large bowl, stir to combine ground lamb, parsley, chopped rosemary, garlic salt, garam masala, and pepper. Wet your hands to prevent sticking and form into 16 meatballs. Alternately thread olives and meatballs onto the rosemary stalks.

3. Brush grate with *oil*. Grill skewers for 12 to 15 minutes or until lamb is cooked, turning often. Serve with pita and tzatziki.

WHITE RUSSIAN

Makes 1 drink

- 1 ounce white crème de cacao
- ½ ounce sweet herbal liqueur
- ½ ounce orange liqueur, *Grand Marnier®*
- 1 splash orange juice
- 2 scoops vanilla ice cream

In a blender, combine white crème de cacao, herbal liqueur, orange liqueur, and orange juice. Add ice cream. Cover and blend until thick and creamy. Serve.

CRANBERRY MARGARITA

Makes 1 drink

- ¼   cup whole cranberry sauce
- 1½   ounces cranberry juice
- 1   ounce tequila, *Jose Cuervo Especial®*
- ½   ounce orange liqueur, *Grand Marnier®*
- 10   ice cubes

In a blender, combine all ingredients. Cover and blend on high until slushy. Pour into prepared glass. Garnish.

CITRUS SOOTHER

Makes 1 drink

- 3   ounces cranberry juice
- 1½   ounces citrus flavored vodka, *Smirnoff®*
-     Lemon wedge, nectarine wedge, lychee nuts

Fill glass with ice. Add cranberry juice and vodka. Stir and garnish.

ARUGULA SALAD

Start to Finish 10 minutes   **Makes** 6 servings

- 1   package (8-ounce) arugula
- 1   cup grape tomatoes, halved
- ½   cup canned whole kernel corn, drained, *Libby's®*
- 3   tablespoons olive oil and vinegar dressing
-     Shaved Parmesan cheese

1. In a large bowl, combine arugula, tomatoes, and corn. Pour dressing over arugula mixture. Toss to coat. Divide among serving plates and garnish with Parmesan cheese.

MANGO BEACH COCKTAIL

Makes 1 drink

- ½ **cup frozen chopped mango**
- ¼ **cup vanilla fat-free yogurt**
- ¼ **cup mango nectar**
- 1½ **ounces tequila,** *Jose Cuervo Especial*®
- **Crushed ice, peach slices**

In a blender, combine mango, yogurt, mango nectar, and tequila. Cover and blend on high until smooth and frothy. Pour into an ice-filled glass. Garnish with peach slices.

RED PEPPER MEATBALLS

Prep 30 minutes   **Bake** 10 minutes   **Makes** 6 servings

FOR ZESTY FRIED MEATBALLS

- **No-stick cooking spray,** *Pam*®
- 1 **pound lean ground beef**
- 4 **eggs**
- 1 **cup seasoned fine dry bread crumbs,** *Progresso*®
- ¾ **cup shredded Parmesan cheese,** *Sargento*®
- ¼ **cup milk**
- 1 **teaspoon dried Italian seasoning,** *McCormick*®
- 1 **tablespoon water**
- 2 **cups vegetable oil or peanut oil,** *Wesson*®

FOR RED PEPPER SAUCE

- 1 **jar (7¼-ounce) roasted red peppers, drained,** *Delallo*®
- ½ **cup Catalina salad dressing,** *Kraft*®
- 1 **teaspoon dried Italian seasoning,** *McCormick*®
- **Fresh thyme sprigs**

1. For Zesty Fried Meatballs: Preheat oven to 425 degrees F. Coat a rimmed baking sheet with cooking spray. In a bowl, combine ground beef, 3 eggs, ¾ cup bread crumbs, Parmesan cheese, milk, and Italian seasoning. Form into 1-inch meatballs. In a bowl, beat together 1 egg and water. Place ¼ cup bread crumbs in another bowl. Dip meatballs into egg mixture, then roll in bread crumbs.

2. In a heavy saucepan, heat oil over high heat. Working in batches, add meatballs to hot oil. Fry until golden brown. Remove meatballs; drain well. Arrange in a single layer on baking sheet. Bake for 10 to 15 minutes or until cooked through (160 degrees F). For Red Pepper Sauce: In a blender, combine roasted peppers, salad dressing, and Italian seasoning. Cover and blend until smooth. Serve meatballs with sauce. Garnish with fresh thyme.

august

blue cosmo ten midori passion
fruit martini peach drop cîroc
blue ocean ten blue lagoon
heirloom sangria mixed-berry
daiquiri florence fizzy peachy
margarita blue seafoam blue
hawaiian blue cosmo ten midori
passion fruit martini peach
drop cîroc blue ocean ten blue
lagoon heirloom sangria mixed

TEN MIDORI

Makes 1 drink

- 1¼ ounces gin, *Tanqueray No. TEN®*
- 1 ounce lime juice
- 1 splash melon liqueur
- 1 cup ice cubes
-   Maraschino cherry

In a blender, combine gin, lime juice, and melon liqueur. Add ice. Cover and blend until slushy. Pour into a chilled glass. Garnish with cherry.

APPLE AND BRIE QUESADILLAS

Prep 15 minutes   **Cook** 5 minutes   **Makes** 4 servings

FOR GRILLED APPLE AND BRIE QUESADILLAS

- ¼ cup cream cheese, *Philadelphia®*
- 8 flour tortillas (6-inch), *Mission®*
- 8 ounces Brie cheese, cut into thin strips
- 1 apple, thinly sliced
-   No-stick cooking spray, *Pam®*

FOR STRAWBERRY-APPLE DIPPING SAUCE

- 1 jar (8-ounce) strawberry jam
- ¼ cup applesauce
- 1 pinch ground cinnamon

1. For Grilled Apple and Brie Quesadillas: Spread cream cheese on 4 tortillas. Place Brie and apples on top. Place remaining tortillas on top.

2. Coat a grill pan with cooking spray. Heat pan over medium-high heat. Add quesadillas. Cook for 5 to 6 minutes or until lightly browned, turning halfway through cooking.

3. For Strawberry-Apple Dipping Sauce: In a microwave-safe bowl, combine all ingredients. Microwave, uncovered, 1 to 2 minutes on high or until hot. Cut quesadillas into wedges. Serve with sauce.

BLUE COSMO

Makes 1 drink

- 1 ounce citrus vodka, *Ketel One Citroen®*
- 1 ounce white cranberry juice
- ½ ounce blue curaçao
- 1 squeeze lime juice
-   Ice cubes

In a cocktail shaker, combine all ingredients; cover and shake until very cold. Strain into a chilled glass.

PEACH DROP

Makes 1 drink

- 1½ ounces lemon drop cocktail mixer, *Stirrings*®
- 1½ ounces citrus flavored vodka, *Smirnoff*®
  Ice cubes
- 1 slice fresh peach

In a cocktail shaker, combine mixer and vodka. Add ice; cover and shake until very cold. Strain into a chilled glass. Garnish with peach.

HERB CHEESE TENDERLOIN

Prep 25 minutes   **Roast** 25 minutes   **Makes** 8 servings

- 2 tablespoons extra virgin olive oil, *Bertolli*®
- 1 1- to 1½ pound premarinated apple bourbon pork tenderloin, *Hormel*®
- 24 to 30 ½-inch-thick slices baguette-style French bread
- 1 package (5.2-ounce) semisoft cheese with garlic and herbs, *Boursin*®
- 12 to 15 cherry tomatoes, cut in half

1. Preheat oven to 425 degrees F. In an ovenproof skillet, heat oil and brown pork on all sides. Place skillet in oven. Roast 25 minutes or until internal temperature reaches 155 degrees F.

2. Place bread on a baking sheet. Bake 5 minutes or until toasted. Spread with 1 heaping teaspoon cheese. Cut pork into 24 slices and place on top of bread. Top with cheese and tomato halves.

PASSION FRUIT MARTINI

Makes 1 drink

- 1½ ounces citrus flavored vodka, *Smirnoff*®
- 1½ ounces white cranberry juice
- 1½ ounces passion fruit juice
- ¼ ounce orange liqueur, *Grand Marnier*®

In a cocktail shaker, combine all ingredients. Add ice; cover and shake until very cold. Strain into a chilled martini glass. Garnish.

BLUE LAGOON

Makes 1 drink

> **Superfine sugar**
> ¾ **ounce gin,** *Tanqueray No. TEN®*
> ¼ **ounce vodka,** *Smirnoff No. 21*™
> ¼ **ounce blue curaçao**
> 1 **splash lime juice**

Wet the rim of a chilled glass with water. Dip rim in sugar. In a cocktail shaker, combine remaining ingredients; add ice cubes. Cover and shake. Strain into glass.

LAS CHALUPAS

Prep 15 minutes   **Cook** 20 minutes   **Makes** 4 servings

> 1 **pound ground beef**
> ⅔ **cup salsa,** *Pace®*
> ¼ **cup jalapeño juice, from bottled jalapeño chile peppers**
> 1 **package (1.25-ounce) taco seasoning mix,** *Ortega®*
> ¼ **cup canola oil,** *Wesson®*
> 4 **flour tortillas (8-inch),** *Mission®*
> ½ **cup shredded Mexican cheese blend,** *Kraft®*
> **Assorted toppings, such as shredded lettuce, chopped tomatoes, sliced olives, guacamole, and sour cream**

1. In a large skillet, brown beef over medium heat. Stir in salsa, jalapeño juice, and taco seasoning. Reduce heat to low and cook, uncovered, for 10 minutes more.

2. Preheat broiler. In another skillet, heat oil over medium-high heat. Fry tortillas until crispy on both sides. Place tortillas on ovenproof plates. Cover each tortilla with meat. Sprinkle with cheese.

3. Broil 6 inches from heat about 2 minutes or until cheese melts. Remove plates. Top with assorted toppings, such as shredded lettuce, tomatoes, olives, guacamole, and sour cream.

CÎROC BLUE OCEAN

Makes 1 drink

> **Crushed ice**
> 1 **ounce vodka,** *Cîroc®*
> ½ **ounce blue curaçao**
> ¼ **ounce grapefruit juice**
> 1 **splash sugar syrup**
> **Thin lemon or orange slice**

Fill a cocktail shaker with crushed ice. Add vodka, blue curaçao, grapefruit juice, and sugar syrup. Cover and shake vigorously. Strain into a glass. Garnish with lemon or orange slice.

MIXED-BERRY DAIQUIRI

Makes 1 drink

1	cup crushed ice
3	ounces frozen mixed berries
1¾	ounces sweet-and-sour mix
1¼	ounces spiced rum, *Captain Morgan® Original Spiced Rum*
	Fresh mixed berries

In a blender, combine ice, frozen berries, sweet-and-sour mix, and rum. Cover and blend until smooth. Pour into a chilled glass. Garnish with fresh berries. Serve with a straw.

RICOTTA BERRY BURSTS

Prep 15 minutes   **Bake** 5 minutes   **Makes** 6 tarts

1	package (4-ounce) purchased graham cracker crumb tart shells (6), *Keebler®*
1	egg white
¾	cup boysenberry jam, *Knott's Berry Farm®*
1	container (14-ounce) whole-milk ricotta cheese
1	tablespoon orange juice, *Minute Maid®*
	Fresh boysenberries or blackberries

1. Preheat oven to 375 degrees F. Brush shells with egg white. Bake about 5 minutes or until golden. Transfer shells to a wire rack; cool.

2. In a microwave-safe bowl, heat ¼ cup jam, covered, for 30 seconds or until melted on high (100 percent power). Divide melted jam among shells. In blender, combine ½ cup jam, ricotta cheese, and orange juice. Cover and blend until smooth. Divide mixture among shells. Serve immediately or cover tightly and chill for up to 8 hours. Garnish with fresh berries.

HEIRLOOM SANGRIA

Makes 12 drinks

1	bottle (946-milliliter) red sangria cocktail mixer, chilled, *Stirrings®*
1	bottle (750-milliliter) red wine, chilled, *Beaulieu Vineyard®*
	Sliced fresh fruits, such as oranges, strawberries, and lemons

In a large pitcher, combine cocktail mixer and wine. Pour into 12 chilled glasses. Garnish each with orange, strawberry, and lemon slices.

PEACHY MARGARITA

Makes 1 drink

1	can (8½-ounce) sliced peaches in heavy syrup, *Del Monte®*
3	ounces lime margarita drink mix
1½	ounces tequila, *Jose Cuervo Especial®*
4	ounces crushed ice
	Edible pansy

In a blender, combine undrained peaches, margarita drink mix, and tequila. Add crushed ice. Cover and blend until smooth. Pour into prepared glass. Garnish with edible pansy.

GRILLED LIME BUTTER BREAD

Start to Finish 15 minutes   **Makes** about 16 (2-inch) pieces

2	sticks (1 cup) unsalted butter, at room temperature
1	tablespoon lime juice, *ReaLime®*
2	teaspoons dried chili-lime seasoning, *McCormick®*
1	loaf French bread, cut in half lengthwise

1. In a small bowl, combine butter, lime juice, and chili-lime seasoning; mix well. Using a table knife, lightly spread cut sides of bread with the lime butter.

2. Heat a grill pan over medium-high heat. Place bread, buttered sides down, in pan, cutting to fit if necessary. Cook about 4 minutes or until bread is hot and toasted. Cut bread into 2-inch pieces.

FLORENCE FIZZY

Makes 1 drink

2	ounces peach nectar, *Kern's®*
	Prosecco, *Stellina di Notte®*
	Peach wedge

Pour peach nectar into a champagne flute. Fill with Prosecco. Garnish with peach wedge.

BLUE HAWAIIAN

Makes 1 drink

1	ounce tequila, *Don Julio® Blanco*
½	ounce vodka, *Cîroc®*
1	splash blue curaçao
	Ice cubes
	Tonic water

In a cocktail shaker, combine all ingredients except tonic; cover and shake. Strain into chilled glass. Top with tonic.

CHORIZO TAQUITOS

Prep 20 minutes   **Bake** 18 minutes   **Makes** 12 pieces

1	package (16-ounce) chorizo sausage, casings removed
1	cup medium chunky salsa, drained, *Pace®*
1	cup shredded mild cheddar cheese, *Kraft®*
6	fajita-size flour tortillas (8-inch), *Mission®*
1	cup purchased guacamole
¼	cup sour cream

1. Preheat oven to 400 degrees F. Line a baking sheet with foil.

2. Cook sausage over medium heat 6 minutes or until brown. Drain fat; discard. Cool sausage slightly. Stir salsa and cheese into sausage.

3. Place 1 tortilla on a work surface. Spoon ¼ cup of the sausage down center of tortilla. Fold tortilla in half; roll up. Secure with toothpicks. Place on baking sheet. Repeat with tortillas and sausage.

4. Bake 18 minutes or until filling is hot and tortillas are golden brown. Cut in half crosswise. Serve with guacamole and sour cream.

BLUE SEAFOAM

Makes 1 drink

	Ice cubes
¾	ounce blueberry flavored vodka, *Smirnoff®*
¾	ounce vanilla flavored vodka, *Smirnoff®*
1	splash blue curaçao
	Fresh blueberries

Fill a cocktail shaker with ice. Add blueberry vodka, vanilla vodka, and curaçao; shake well. Pour into a chilled glass. Garnish.

september

santa fe coolers apple sour
mango madras decadent
sippers beer buffet benefit
fashionable phyllis rio rum
punch happy homemaker
iced brownie espresso apple
sour santa fe coolers mango
madras decadent sippers
beer buffet benefit rio rum
punch fashionable phyllis

SANTE FE COOLERS

Prep 10 minutes   **Stand** 20 minutes   **Makes** 12 drinks

1	2-inch piece fresh ginger, sliced
2	cups water
1	can (12-ounce) frozen lemonade concentrate
1	bottle (12-ounce) beer, *Red Stripe®*
3½	cups ginger ale, *Canada Dry®*
1½	cups vodka, *Cîroc®*
	Ice cubes, lime slices (optional)

In a small saucepan, bring sliced ginger and water to a boil. Remove from heat and let stand for 20 minutes. Strain, reserving ginger water. In a large pitcher, stir to combine thawed lemonade concentrate, ginger water, beer, ginger ale, and vodka. Pour in glasses over ice. Garnish with lime slices (optional).

HALIBUT SALSA TACOS

Prep 15 minutes   **Stand** 30 minutes
Grill 8 minutes   **Makes** 8 servings

1	packet (1-ounce) hot taco seasoning, *Lawry's®*
1	pound fresh halibut
2	cups mild chunky salsa, *Newman's Own®*
1	cup frozen peach slices, chopped and thawed, *Dole®*
1	teaspoon ground allspice, *McCormick®*
1	package (8-ounce) coleslaw mix, *Ready Pac®*
8	corn tortillas (6-inch), *Mission®*

1. Set up grill for direct cooking over medium heat. When ready to grill, brush grate with *oil*. Sprinkle taco seasoning over halibut; rub in with your fingers. Let stand for 30 minutes.

2. Grill halibut, covered, about 8 minutes or just until fish flakes when tested with fork. Let cool. Cut into bite-size pieces.

3. In a medium bowl, combine salsa, peaches, and allspice. Divide halibut among warm tortillas. Top with salsa and coleslaw mix.

MANGO MADRAS

Makes 1 drink

- 2 **ounces cranberry juice,** *Ocean Spray*®
- 2 **ounces orange juice**
- 1½ **ounces mango rum,** *Captain Morgan*® *Parrot Bay Mango*
- **Ice cubes**
- **Orange wedges**
- **Maraschino cherries**

In a glass, combine cranberry juice, orange juice, and rum. Add ice. Garnish with orange wedges and maraschino cherries.

SMOKY TOMATO SALAD

Start to Finish 20 minutes   **Makes** 6 servings

FOR PARMESAN VINAIGRETTE
- ½ **cup olive oil-and-vinegar salad dressing**
- ¼ **cup grated Parmesan cheese,** *DiGiorno*®
- 2 **teaspoons Dijon mustard,** *Grey Poupon*®
- 3 **drops liquid smoke**

FOR TOMATO SALAD
- 6 **medium tomatoes, cut into chunks**
- 8 **ounces fresh mozzarella, torn in pieces,** *Cantaré*®
- 15 **fresh basil leaves, finely chopped**
- **Salt and pepper**

1. For Parmesan Vinaigrette: In a medium bowl whisk together salad dressing, Parmesan cheese, mustard, and liquid smoke.

3. For Tomato Salad: In a salad bowl, combine tomatoes, mozzarella cheese, and basil. Pour Parmesan Vinaigrette over salad and toss to coat. Season with salt and pepper to taste. Serve immediately.

DECADENT SIPPERS

Makes 3 drinks

CHOCOLATE HEAVEN

1	ounce vanilla flavored vodka, *Smirnoff*®
1	cup chocolate or mocha smoothie
2	tablespoons simple or sugar syrup
	Club soda, *Schweppes*®

BLUSHING PEONIES

1	ounce strawberry flavored vodka, *Smirnoff*®
1	cup strawberry smoothie
2	tablespoons simple syrup
	Club soda, *Schweppes*®

TROPICAL VISION

1	ounce mango rum, *Captain Morgan Parrot Bay*® *Mango*
1	cup mango smoothie
2	tablespoons simple syrup
	Club soda, *Schweppes*®

In a glass filled with ice, add the vodka or rum, smoothie, and syrup. Top with club soda; stir.

BEER BUFFET BENEFIT

Makes 8 servings

8	12-ounce bottles of lager-style beer, *Red Stripe®*
	Orange-flavor liqueur, *Grand Marnier®*
	Mango rum, *Captain Morgan Parrot Bay® Mango*
	Coffee Irish cream liqueur, *Baileys®*
	Strawberry flavored vodka, *Smirnoff®*
	Melon-flavor liqueur
	Passion fruit syrup, *Torani®*
	Tomato juice
	Hot pepper sauce, *Tabasco®*
	Worcestershire sauce

Orange-Spiked Beer: Add 1 ounce of orange-flavor liqueur to 12 ounces of beer.

Mango-Spiked Beer: Add 1 ounce of mango rum to 12 ounces of beer.

Beer Buzz: Add 1 ounce of coffee Irish cream liqueur to 12 ounces of beer.

Beer Passion: Add 1 ounce passion fruit syrup to 12 ounces of beer.

Red Eye: Add 1 ounce of tomato juice to 12 ounces of beer.

Beer Mary: Add 1 ounce of tomato juice, several drops of hot pepper sauce, and a splash of Worcestershire sauce to 12 ounces of beer.

Sound Wind: Add 1 ounce of strawberry vodka to 12 ounces of beer.

Smooth Sailing: Add 1 ounce of melon liqueur to 12 ounces of beer.

GREEK GARLIC FRIES

Start to Finish 10 minutes   **Makes** 4 servings

½	bag (26-ounce) frozen "fast food" fries, *Ore-Ida®*
2	tablespoons extra virgin olive oil
1½	teaspoons bottled crushed garlic, *Christopher Ranch®*
1	teaspoon Greek seasoning, *Spice Islands®*
	Tzatziki or gyro dressing

1. Preheat broiler.

2. On a heavy-duty baking sheet, toss together fries, olive oil, garlic, and Greek seasoning. Arrange fries in a single layer.

3. Broil 6 inches from heat for 5 to 8 minutes or until golden brown. Serve fries hot with tzatziki for dipping.

FASHIONABLE PHYLLIS

Makes 1 drink

1½ ounces Canadian whisky, *Crown Royal*®
3 ounces orange juice
1 tablespoon grenadine
Maraschino cherry
Orange slice

In an ice-filled glass, combine whisky, orange juice, and grenadine. Garnish with cherry and orange slice.

RIO RUM PUNCH

Makes 12 servings

3 cups peach nectar, chilled, *Kern's*®
2 cups frozen peaches, *Dole*®
2 cups spiced rum, chilled, *Captain Morgan*®
  Original Spiced Rum
1 cup unsweetened pineapple juice, chilled, *Dole*®
1 cup ginger ale, chilled, *Schweppes*®
Peach slices

In a punch bowl, combine peach nectar, peaches, rum, and pineapple juice. Add ginger ale. Garnish with peach slices.

CHOCOLATE FONDUE BAR

Start to Finish 25 minutes   **Makes** 12 servings

FOR CHOCOLATE-CARAMEL FONDUE

¾   cup whipping cream

3   tablespoons cognac

1   bag (12-ounce) semisweet chocolate chips

½   cup butterscotch caramel sauce

FOR WHITE CHOCOLATE-BERRY FONDUE

¾   cup whipping cream

3   bars (4 ounces each) white chocolate baking bar,
    cut into small pieces

⅔   cup blackberry spreadable fruit

¼   cup amaretto, *Disaronno®*

FOR FONDUE BAR DIPPERS

1   container (14-ounce) brownie bites

1   container (14-ounce) doughnut holes

    Assorted fresh fruit, such as whole strawberries
    and banana chunks

    Nut topping

    Rainbow sprinkles, *Betty Crocker®*

1. For Chocolate-Caramel Fondue: In a small saucepan, heat cream and cognac, over medium heat, just until below a boil. In a medium bowl, add chocolate chips. Pour hot cream-cognac mixture over chocolate chips, stirring with a rubber spatula until completely smooth. Stir in caramel sauce until combined. Transfer mixture to a 1½-quart slow cooker to keep warm or cover with plastic wrap and store until ready to serve.

2. For White Chocolate-Berry Fondue: In a small saucepan, heat cream, over medium heat, just until below a boil. In a medium bowl, add white chocolate pieces. Pour hot cream over white chocolate, stirring with a rubber spatula until completely smooth. Stir in spreadable fruit and amaretto until combined. Transfer mixture to a 1½-quart slow cooker to keep warm or cover with plastic wrap and refrigerate until ready to reheat and serve.

3. For Fondue Bar Dippers: On a serving platter, arrange brownie bites, doughnut holes, and fresh fruit; place cocktail picks nearby. Pour nut topping and rainbow sprinkles into small serving bowls.

4. If necessary, reheat fondues for 5 minutes over low heat. Place warm White Chocolate-Berry Fondue and Chocolate-Caramel Fondue beside dippers. Garnish White Chocolate-Berry Fondue with additional rainbow sprinkles.

ICED BROWNIE ESPRESSO

Makes 2 drinks

1	cup ice cubes
½	cup frozen whipped topping
¼	cup sweetened condensed milk
2	shots fresh brewed espresso or ½ cup very strong coffee
3	ounces Irish cream liqueur, *Baileys*®
3	tablespoons semisweet chocolate chips
2	tablespoons chocolate syrup, *Hershey's*®
	Frozen whipped topping, thawed
	Chocolate syrup, *Hershey's*®

In a blender, combine ice, the ½ cup whipped topping, condensed milk, espresso, Irish cream, chocolate chips, and the 2 tablespoons chocolate syrup. Cover and blend until smooth. Pour into 2 glasses. For garnish, in a pastry bag fitted with a large star tip, spoon in whipped topping. Pipe on top of each drink. Or spoon whipped topping into a small zip-top plastic bag. Snip off one corner of the bag and pipe. Drizzle with chocolate syrup.

APPLE SOUR

Makes 1 drink

- 1¼ **ounces green apple flavored vodka,** *Smirnoff®*
- ¼ **ounce sour mix**

In a cocktail shaker, combine vodka and sour mix. Add ice; cover and shake until very cold. Strain into prepared glass.

BAKED ARTICHOKE DIP

Prep 10 minutes   **Bake** 40 minutes   **Makes** 4 cups

- **No-stick cooking spray,** *Pam®*
- ⅔ **cup fat-free Caesar salad dressing,** *Girard's®*
- ⅓ **cup light mayonnaise,** *Best Foods®/Hellmann's®*
- ⅓ **cup fat-free sour cream,** *Knudsen®*
- ⅓ **cup grated Parmesan cheese,** *DiGiorno®*
- 2 **cans (15 ounces each) artichoke quarters in water, drained and chopped,** *Maria®*
- 1 **can (14.5-ounce) organic diced tomatoes with basil and garlic, drained,** *Muir Glen®*
- 5 **ounces low-fat Swiss cheese, shredded,** *Alpine Lace®*
- ½ **teaspoon hot pepper sauce,** *Tabasco®*
- **Baked tortilla chips and/or vegetable dippers**

1. Preheat oven to 350 degrees F. Coat a 1-quart baking dish with cooking spray; set aside.

2. In a medium bowl, combine all remaining ingredients except tortilla chips and vegetable dippers. Transfer mixture to baking dish. Bake for 40 to 45 minutes or until set and top is golden brown. Serve warm with tortilla chips and/or vegetable dippers.

HAPPY HOMEMAKER

Makes 1 drink

2½   **ounces pineapple juice**

1½   **ounces white rum, *Oronoco*®**

¼   **ounce lime juice**

    Ice cubes

    Fresh mint (optional)

In a cocktail shaker, combine pineapple juice, rum, and lime juice. Add ice; cover and shake until very cold. Strain into a chilled martini glass. Garnish with mint (optional).

october

spiced cider crushed orange
hot strudel passion cosmo
chocolate pumpkin pie cîroc
ola autumn coffee maple
shake vanilla chocotini velvet
cocktail spiced cider crushed
orange hot strudel passion
cosmo chocolate pumpkin
pie cîrocola autumn coffee
maple shake vanilla chocotini

SPICED CIDER

Prep 5 minutes   **Cook** 2 hours (Low)   **Makes** 20 servings

2	cans (11.5 ounces each) peach nectar
2	cans (11.5 ounces each) apricot nectar
3	cups water
1	cup packed brown sugar
1	cup Canadian whisky, *Crown Royal*®
½	cup lemon juice
1	teaspoon ground allspice
2	to 3 cinnamon sticks
1	package (12-ounce) frozen peach slices, thawed

In a 4-quart slow cooker, combine all ingredients except peach slices. Cover and cook on Low heat setting 2 to 3 hours. Remove cinnamon sticks. Serve in mugs. Garnish with peach slices.

CHICKEN CAESAR FOCCACIA

Start to Finish 10 minutes   **Makes** 8 sandwiches

1	package (7.5-ounce) Caesar salad kit, *Fresh Express*®
½	package (6-ounce) grilled chicken strips, chopped, *Oscar Mayer*®
1	loaf focaccia bread
8	4-inch-long fresh rosemary sprigs
8	cherry tomatoes

1. In a large bowl, combine contents of salad kit and chicken strips; toss.

2. Cut focaccia loaf in half horizontally. Fill loaf with chicken Caesar salad mixture. Cut sandwich into 8 portions.

3. Strip leaves from bottom halves of rosemary sprigs, leaving leaves at top. Insert rosemary skewers through cherry tomatoes. Insert one rosemary-tomato skewer into the top of each sandwich.

HOT STRUDEL

Makes 1 drink

3 ounces hot apple cider
¼ ounce peppermint
schnapps, *Rumple Minze*®

In a heatproof cup, stir together cider
and peppermint schnapps. Garnish with
cinnamon stick and apple wedge.

CHOCOLATE PUMPKIN PIE

Makes 1 drink

¾ ounce vanilla flavored vodka, *Smirnoff*®

½ ounce Irish cream liqueur, *Baileys*®

½ ounce coffee liqueur

½ ounce crème de cacao

⅛ teaspoon pumpkin pie spice

Pinch cayenne pepper

Ice cubes

In a cocktail shaker, combine vodka, Irish cream, coffee liqueur, crème de cacao, pumpkin pie spice, and cayenne pepper. Add ice; cover and shake until very cold. Strain into a chilled martini glass.

SAVORY BREAD PUDDING

Prep 25 minutes   **Bake** 35 minutes   **Makes** 12 mini bread puddings

No-stick cooking spray, *Pam*®

8 ounces sweet Italian sausage, *Johnsonville*®

1 package (8-ounce) sliced fresh mushrooms

1 tablespoon canola oil, *Wesson*®

1 teaspoon bottled crushed garlic

2 cups milk

4 eggs

1 teaspoon Italian seasoning, *McCormick*®

½ teaspoon salt

¼ teaspoon freshly ground black pepper

½ loaf country-style bread, cut into 1-inch cubes

1. Preheat oven to 325 degrees F. Coat twelve 2½-inch muffin cups with cooking spray; set aside.

2. In a large skillet, over medium heat, cook sausage until browned, breaking up lumps. Remove sausage from skillet. Add mushrooms, oil, and garlic to skillet. Cook and stir until mushrooms are lightly browned. Remove from heat and stir in sausage. Let cool.

3. In a large bowl, whisk together milk, eggs, Italian seasoning, salt, and pepper. Add cubed bread and sausage mixture to egg mixture; press bread with back of a large spoon to submerge into milk mixture. Let stand for 10 minutes or until bread absorbs milk mixture. Ladle bread pudding mixture into prepared muffin cups and place in a large rimmed baking pan. Carefully pour hot water into the baking pan. Bake for 35 to 40 minutes or until top is golden brown and bread pudding puffs. Serve warm.

CRUSHED ORANGE

Makes 1 drink

½   **cup ice cubes**

2   **ounces unsweetened pineapple juice**

2   **ounces cranberry juice**

1½   **ounces orange flavored vodka,** *Smirnoff®*

In a blender, combine all ingredients; blend. Pour into chilled glass.

CÎROC LOLA

Makes 1 drink

   Ice cubes

1½   **ounces pomegranate juice**

1   **ounce vodka,** *Cîroc®*

1   **splash Champagne**

   Very thin apple slice

Fill a cocktail shaker with ice. Add pomegranate juice and vodka. Cover and shake vigorously. Strain into a chilled cocktail glass. Top with Champagne. Garnish with apple slice.

CAYENNE CURLY FRIES

Prep 5 minutes   **Bake** 20 minutes   **Makes** 4 servings

1   **package (28-ounce) frozen curly fries,** *Ore-Ida®*

1   **tablespoon extra virgin olive oil**

1   **tablespoon Cajun seasoning**

½   **teaspoon cayenne pepper,** *McCormick®*

Preheat oven to 400 degrees F. In large bowl, combine curly fries, olive oil, Cajun seasoning, and cayenne pepper; toss until fries are well coated. Transfer to a baking sheet. Bake for 20 minutes.

PASSION COSMO

Makes 1 drink

1½	ounces passion fruit flavored vodka, *Smirnoff®*
¼	ounce Triple Sec or orange liqueur
1	splash lime juice
1	splash cranberry juice
	Ice cubes, lime twist

In a cocktail shaker, combine vodka, Triple Sec, lime juice, and cranberry juice. Add ice; cover and shake until very cold. Strain into a chilled martini glass. Garnish with lime twist.

SMOKED SALMON-AND-OLIVE BLINI

Prep 15 minutes   **Cook** 3 minutes per batch   **Makes** 32 blini

1	cup buckwheat pancake and waffle mix, *Aunt Jemima®*
1	cup whole milk
1	egg
1	tablespoon vegetable oil, *Wesson®*
	No-stick cooking spray, *Pam®*
6	ounces sliced smoked salmon or lox, *Vita®*
¾	cup kalamata olive spread, *Peloponnese®*
¾	cup light sour cream, *Knudsen®*
	Fresh dill, chopped
	Chopped ripe olives, *Early California®*

1. In a medium bowl, beat together pancake mix, milk, egg, and oil until just blended. Set aside.

2. Coat griddle with nonstick cooking spray. Heat griddle over medium heat.

3. Drop batter by tablespoonfuls onto griddle. Cook for 2 minutes or until bubbles appear; turn blini over. Cook for 1 minute more. Set aside. Repeat with remaining batter.

4. Cut salmon into 32 pieces. Spread each blini with some of the olive spread. Arrange on a platter. Top each with a piece of smoked salmon and 1 teaspoon sour cream. Sprinkle with dill and olives.

AUTUMN COFFEE

Makes 1 drink

1	ounce mocha liqueur, *Godiva*®
⅔	cup hot coffee
1	tablespoon chocolate syrup, *Hershey's*®

In a heatproof glass combine mocha liqueur, coffee, and chocolate syrup. Stir and serve.

MAPLE SHAKE

Makes 2 shakes

2	cups light butter pecan ice cream
⅔	cup low-fat milk
2	tablespoons maple-flavored syrup
1	teaspoon almond extract

In a blender, combine ice cream, milk, syrup, and almond extract. Cover and blend about 1 minute or until smooth. Pour into tall glasses and serve with straws.

CHEESY CHILI FRIES

Prep 15 minutes   **Cook** 30 minutes   **Bake** 25 minutes
Makes 8 to 10 servings

1	pound ground beef
1	bottle (12-ounce) chili sauce, *Heinz*®
½	cup water
1	packet (1.48-ounce) chili seasoning mix, *Lawry's*®
1	tablespoon yellow mustard, *French's*®
1	teaspoon Worcestershire sauce
½	teaspoon onion powder
1	bag (32-ounce) frozen crinkle-cut french-fry potatoes, *Ore-Ida*® *Golden Crinkles*®
	Shredded cheddar cheese, *Kraft*®

1. Preheat oven to 450 degrees F. Line a baking sheet with aluminum foil.

2. In a large saucepan, over medium heat, brown ground beef, stirring frequently to break up meat in fine pieces. Add chili sauce, water, dry chili seasoning mix, mustard, Worcestershire sauce, and onion powder. Bring to a boil; reduce heat. Simmer, uncovered, for 30 minutes.

3. Meanwhile, arrange crinkle fries on prepared baking sheet in a single layer. Bake for 25 to 30 minutes or until golden and crispy. Arrange on serving plate. Spoon ground beef mixture over the top. Sprinkle with shredded cheese.

VANILLA CHOCOTINI

Makes 1 drink

1	ounce chocolate liqueur, *Godiva®*
¼	ounce vanilla flavored vodka, *Smirnoff®*

In a cocktail shaker, combine chocolate liqueur and vodka. Add ice; cover and shake until very cold. Pour into chilled martini glass.

GUINNESS CHEDDAR FONDUE

Prep 5 minutes   **Cook** 3 hours (Low)   **Makes** 12 servings

4	cups shredded cheddar cheese, *Kraft®*
2	cans (10.75 ounces each) condensed cheddar soup, *Campbell's®*
1	bottle (12-ounce) stout, *Guinness®*
2	teaspoons Worcestershire sauce
1	teaspoon bottled garlic juice, *McCormick®*
1	teaspoon dry English mustard, *Colman's®*
1	loaf dense whole grain bread, cut into cubes

1. Reserve some of the cheese for garnish. In a 4-quart slow cooker, combine remaining cheese, soup, stout, Worcestershire sauce, garlic juice, and mustard.

2. Cover and cook on Low heat setting for 3 to 4 hours, stirring occasionally. Garnish with reserved cheese. Serve with bread.

VELVET COCKTAIL

Makes 4 drinks

1   can (15-ounce) stout beer, chilled, *Guinness®*
1   bottle (12-ounce) hard cider, chilled

Divide the beer between 4 glasses. Invert a spoon over the top of a glass and gently pour some of the cider on top of the beer. Repeat with remaining glasses.

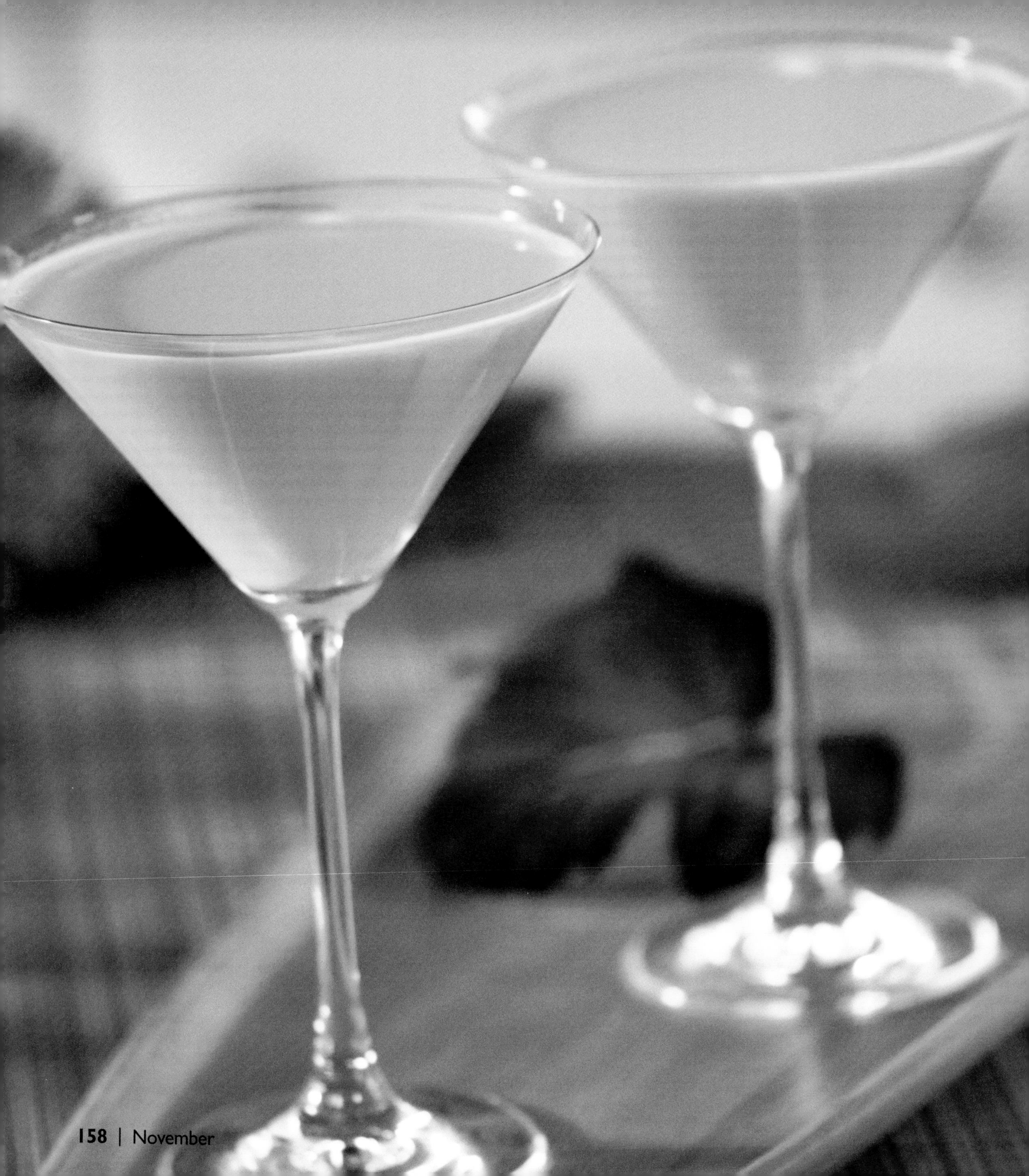

november

rockefeller martini zen-gria
knight delight dream martini
ginito perfect alibi scottish
screwdriver best ever hot
chocolate peach and apricot
cider bountiful harvest
golden old fashioned café à
orange choc-o-mint martini
rockefeller martini zen-gria
knight delight dream martini
ginito perfect alibi scottish

ROCKEFELLER MARTINI

Makes 1 drink

1	tablespoon sugar
1	teaspoon ground cinnamon
1½	ounces cranberry juice
1	ounce vodka, *Smirnoff No. 21*™
¼	ounce cinnamon schnapps, *Goldschläger*®
¼	ounce orange liqueur, *Grand Marnier*®
	Ice cubes
	Cinnamon stick

In a shallow bowl, combine sugar and cinnamon. Dampen rim of a chilled martini glass with *water* and dip in sugar mixture. Set aside. In a cocktail shaker, combine cranberry juice, vodka, cinnamon schnapps, and orange liqueur. Add ice; cover and shake until very cold. Strain into prepared glass. Garnish with cinnamon stick.

ZEN-GRIA

Makes 10 servings

1½	cups white wine, *Beaulieu Vineyard*®
2	bags green tea with honey
1	cup frozen dark sweet cherries
1	can (10.4-ounce) mandarin oranges in juice
1	cup canned lychees, ½ cup juice reserved
1	bottle (750-milliliter) plum wine, chilled
	Orange peel curls

In a small saucepan, heat white wine over high heat just until simmering. Reduce heat to low and add tea bags. Steep for 5 minutes. Remove from heat and cool completely. In a large pitcher, combine frozen cherries, mandarin oranges with juice, and lychees with reserved juice. Add cooled green tea-white wine mixture. Add plum wine. Serve cold in wineglasses. Garnish with orange peel curls.

BEST EVER HOT CHOCOLATE

Makes 2 drinks

1	cup half-and-half
¼	cup milk chocolate chips
¼	teaspoon ground cinnamon
1½	ounces vanilla flavored vodka, *Smirnoff®*

In a saucepan, combine half-and-half, chocolate chips, and cinnamon. Heat over medium heat for 5 minutes or until chocolate is melted, stirring frequently. (Do not boil.) Pour into mug. Stir in vodka.

KNIGHT DELIGHT

Makes 1 drink

1	ounce white chocolate liqueur, *Godiva®*
1	ounce half-and-half
1	ounce orange liqueur, *Grand Marnier®*
	Ice cubes

In a cocktail shaker, combine white chocolate liqueur, half-and-half, and orange liqueur. Add ice; cover and shake until very cold. Strain into a chilled glass.

DREAM MARTINI

Makes 1 drink

	Sugar
1	ounce black cherry flavored vodka, *Smirnoff®*
1	ounce mocha liqueur, *Godiva®*
½	ounce milk
1	splash grenadine
	Ice cubes

Wet rim of a chilled martini glass with *water*. Dip rim in sugar. Set aside. In a cocktail shaker, combine vodka, mocha liqueur, milk, grenadine, and ice. Cover; shake until very cold. Strain into glass.

PERFECT ALIBI

Makes 1 drink

> Ice cubes
> 1 ounce gin, *Tanqueray*®
> ½ ounce sweet vermouth
> ½ ounce bitter Italian apéritif
> 1 splash orange juice
> Orange slice

Fill a cocktail shaker with ice. Add gin, sweet vermouth, apéritif, and orange juice. Cover and shake vigorously. Strain into an ice-filled glass. Garnish with an orange slice.

STUFFED CRESCENTS

Prep 15 minutes   **Bake** 20 minutes   **Makes** 8 servings

> 1 package (8-ounce) refrigerated crescent rolls (8), *Pillsbury*®
> 6 tablespoons shredded sharp cheddar cheese, *Kraft*®
> 6 tablespoons shredded Parmesan cheese, *Kraft*®
> 6 tablespoons semisoft cheese with toasted onion, *Alouette*®
> Fresh parsley sprigs

1. Preheat oven to 350 degrees F. Separate crescent rolls. Lay out dough for each roll on a clean flat surface. Fill 3 of the rolls with 2 tablespoons each of cheddar cheese, 2 of the rolls with 3 tablespoons each of the Parmesan cheese, and the remaining 3 rolls with 2 tablespoons each of the semisoft cheese. Starting from the wide end, roll up each crescent roll to enclose filling.

2. Place rolls, point sides down, on an ungreased baking sheet. Bake about 20 minutes or until golden brown. Cut each roll in half and serve hot. Garnish with parsley.

GINITO

Makes 10 drinks

> 2 cups gin, *Tanqueray*®
> 1 cup chilled pomegranate juice
> 1 cup chilled cranberry juice
> 6 packets sugar substitute
> 6 tablespoons lime juice
> Ice cubes, club soda

In a pitcher, combine gin, pomegranate juice, cranberry juice, sugar substitute, and lime juice. Pour into glasses. Add ice. Top with club soda.

BOUNTIFUL HARVEST

Makes 1 drink

1½	ouncees apple juice
1	ounce Scotch, *Johnnie Walker® Black Label®*
½	ounce peach liqueur
¼	ounce freshly squeezed lemon juice

In a tall glass, combine all ingredients. Add *ice*.

SCOTTISH SCREWDRIVER

Makes 1 drink

1	ounce Scotch, *Johnnie Walker® Red Label®*
1	ounce orange juice
½	ounce green apple flavored vodka, *Smirnoff®*

In a cocktail shaker, combine Scotch, orange juice, and vodka. Add *ice*; cover and shake until very cold. Pour into a chilled glass.

PESTO BREAD

Prep 10 minutes **Bake** 15 minutes **Makes** 6 servings

¼	cup pesto, *Classico®*
6	cloves bottled roasted garlic
1	loaf Italian bread, halved horizontally

Preheat oven to 350 degrees F. In a bowl, combine pesto and garlic, mashing garlic until mixture is smooth. Spread the cut sides of the Italian bread with pesto-garlic mixture. Reassemble loaf. Wrap loaf in aluminum foil. Bake for 15 minutes. Remove foil. Slice and serve.

CAFE À L'ORANGE

Prep 10 minutes   **Cook** 2 hours (Low)   **Makes** 12 drinks

6	cups water
⅔	cup sugar
½	cup chocolate liqueur, *Godiva*®
½	cup orange liqueur, *Grand Marnier*®
6	tablespoons instant coffee crystals
2	tablespoons unsweetened cocoa powder, *Hershey's*®
2	cups half-and-half
1	teaspoon orange extract
1	container (8-ounce) frozen whipped topping
	Unsweetened cocoa powder
	Orange peel curls

In a 4-quart slow cooker, stir together the water, sugar, chocolate liqueur, orange liqueur, coffee crystals, and the 2 tablespoons cocoa powder. Cover and heat on Low heat setting for 2 to 3 hours. Stir in half-and-half. Turn slow cooker to Warm setting. Stir orange extract into whipped topping. Serve liqueur mixture in Irish coffee mugs. Top each with a dollop of whipped topping. Sprinkle cocoa powder. Garnish with orange peel curls.

PEACH AND APRICOT CIDER

Prep 10 minutes   **Cook** 2 hours (Low)   **Makes** 10 drinks

2	cans (11.5 ounces each) peach nectar
2	cans (11.5 ounces each) apricot nectar
1	bag (12-ounce) frozen peach slices
3	cups water
1	cup packed light brown sugar
1	cup bourbon, *Bulleit*®
½	cup lemon juice
1	teaspoon ground allspice
2	cinnamon sticks
	Cinnamon stick

In a 4-quart slow cooker, combine peach nectar, apricot nectar, peach slices, the water, brown sugar, bourbon, lemon juice, allspice, and 2 cinnamon sticks. Cover and heat on Low heat setting for 2 to 3 hours. Discard cinnamon sticks. Turn slow cooker to Warm heat setting. Serve in mugs with additional cinnamon sticks.

GOLDEN OLD-FASHIONED

Makes 1 drink

1½	ounces Canadian whisky, *Crown Royal*®
1	sugar cube
1	teaspoon water
1	dash bitters
	Splash of pineapple juice
	Ice cubes
	Maraschino cherry
	Orange slice

In a glass, combine whisky, sugar cube, water, bitters, and pineapple juice. Using a spoon stir until sugar is dissolved. Add ice cubes. Garnish with cherry and orange slice.

CHOCO-MINT MARTINI

Makes 1 drink

2	ounces mint chocolate Irish cream liqueur, *Baileys*®
½	ounce vanilla flavored vodka, *Smirnoff*®
	Ice

In a cocktail shaker, combine Irish cream and vodka. Add ice; cover and shake until very cold. Strain into a chilled martini glass.

DOUBLE RELISH-DIPPED CHEESE RAVIOI

Prep 25 minutes   **Cook** 2 minutes per batch   **Makes** 16 ravioli

FOR TOMATO-PEPPER RELISH

1	cup roasted red peppers, drained and finely chopped, *Mezzetta*®
¼	cup canned diced tomatoes, drained and finely chopped, *S&W*®
1	tablespoon packed brown sugar, *Domino*®/*C&H*®
1	teaspoon balsamic vinegar

FOR ARTICHOKE CAPER DIP

1	jar (6-ounce) marinated artichoke hearts, drained and finely chopped, *Mezzetta*®
2	tablespoons sour cream, *Knudsen*®
1	tablespoon grated Parmesan cheese, *DiGiorno*®
2	teaspoons mayonnaise, *Best Foods*®/*Hellmann's*®
2	teaspoons capers, drained
1	teaspoon lemon juice, *ReaLemon*®

FOR FRIED CHEESE RAVIOLI

| | **Vegetable oil,** *Wesson*® |
| 1 | package (9-ounce) refrigerated four-cheese ravioli, *Buitoni* |

1. For Tomato Pepper Relish: In a small bowl, combine red peppers and tomatoes, brown sugar, and balsamic vinegar; set aside. For artichoke caper dip: In a small bowl, combine artichoke hearts, sour cream, Parmesan cheese, mayonnaise, capers, and lemon juice.

2. For Fried Cheese Ravioli: In a large saucepan, heat 2 inches of vegetable oil over medium-high heat until temperature reaches 350 degrees F. Fry ravioli, a few at a time, about 2 minutes or until golden brown, turning once. Remove ravioli using a slotted spoon. Drain on paper towels. Keep warm in a 300 degrees F oven while cooking remaining ravioli. Serve with relish and dip.

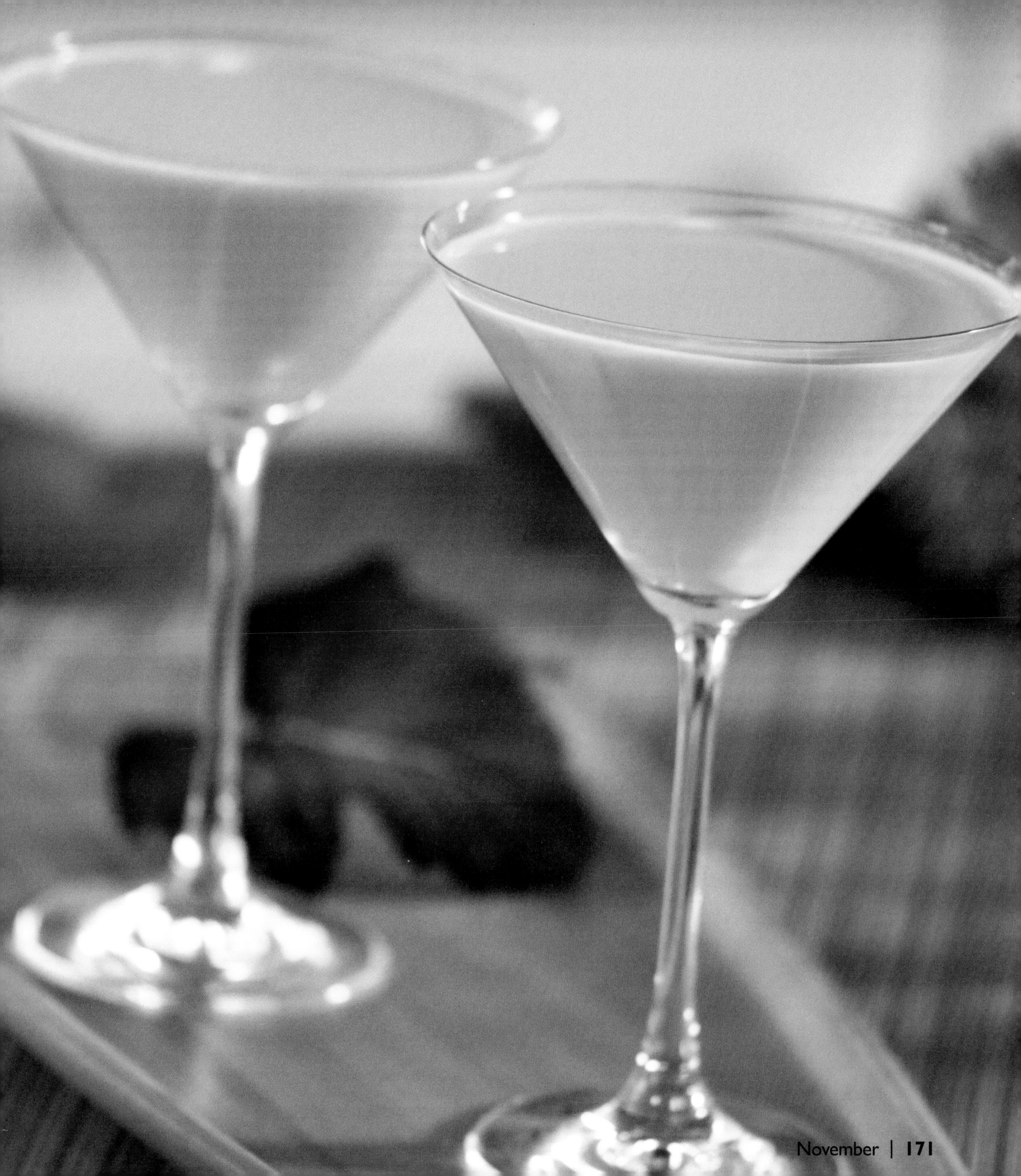

december

snow glacier cocktail coffee
bean russian cream polar
espresso sugarplum rouge
cranberry kiss irish egg nog
pear-y merry martini godiva
truffletini sugarplum rouge
snow glacier cocktail coffee
bean russian cream polar
espresso sugarplum rouge
cranberry kiss irish egg nog
pear-y merry martini godiva

SNOW GLACIER COCKTAIL

Makes 1 drink

    Honey or corn syrup

    Sweetened shredded coconut

1   ounce vodka, *Smirnoff No. 21*™

½   ounce passion fruit liqueur

¼   ounce orange liqueur, *Grand Marnier*®

1   cup ice cubes

Pour honey onto a plate. Place coconut on another plate. Dip the rim of a chilled glass into honey; dip in coconut. Set glass aside. In a blender, combine vodka, passion fruit liqueur, orange liqueur, and ice. Cover and blend until smooth. Pour into prepared glass.

BEST EVER FINGER DOGS

Prep 25 minutes   **Bake** 10 minutes   **Makes** 48 dogs

1   package (48) small cooked smoked beef sausage links

1   container (16.3-ounce) buttermilk biscuits, *Pillsbury*® *Grands*

1   cup shredded cheddar cheese, *Kraft*®

    Mustard or other condiments

1. Preheat oven to 375 degrees F. Line a baking pan with parchment paper or aluminum foil.

2. In a grill pan, cook half of the sausage links over medium heat about 5 minutes or until sausage links are plump. Set aside.

3. On a clean surface, cut each of the biscuits into 6 pieces. Place cheese in a small bowl. Roll each piece of dough in the cheese; shape pieces into balls.

4. Gently stretch each ball to fit a susage link. Partially wrap the dough around the sausage. Arrange finger dogs 1 inch apart on prepared baking pan. Bake for 10 minutes. Serve warm with mustard or other desired condiments.

RUSSIAN CREAM

Makes 1 drink

- 2   teaspoons instant espresso powder, *Medaglia D'Oro®*
- 2   tablespoons hot water
- 1   ounce vanilla flavored vodka, *Smirnoff®*
- ½   ounce Irish cream liqueur, *Baileys®*

In a small bowl, stir espresso powder into the hot water until dissolved. Fill a cocktail shaker with *ice.* Add espresso, vodka, and liqueur. Cover and shake vigorously. Strain into an ice-filled glass.

PESTO CHEESE STRAWS

Prep 30 minutes   **Bake** 12 minutes   **Makes** 40 straws

- 1   package (8-ounce) cream cheese, softened, *Philadelphia®*
- ¼   cup grated Parmesan cheese, *Kraft®*
- 1   egg, lightly beaten
- ¼   teaspoon salt
- 1   package (16-ounce) frozen phyllo dough (40 sheets), thawed, *Athens®*
- 1   stick (½ cup) butter, melted
-      Purchased basil pesto, *Buitoni®*

1. Combine cream cheese, Parmesan, egg, and salt. Spoon mixture into a pastry bag fitted with a ¼-inch-diameter round tip. Set aside.

2. Preheat oven to 375 degrees F. Lay out thawed phyllo dough. (Cover remaining phyllo with plastic wrap to prevent it from drying out.) Working quickly, brush 1 phyllo sheet with butter and pipe cheese filling along long edge of phyllo, stopping ½ inch from each end. Fold ends to enclose filling and roll up phyllo to make a straw. Place on a baking sheet. Repeat with remaining phyllo and filling. Bake for 12 to 15 minutes or until golden. Serve with basil pesto.

COFFEE BEAN

Makes 1 drink

-      **Ice cubes**
- 1   **ounce sambuca, *Romana Sambuca®***
- 1   **ounce coffee Irish cream liqueur, *Baileys®***
- 1   **ounce whipping cream**
-      **Whole coffee beans**

Fill cocktail shaker with ice. Add sambuca, coffee liqueur, and whipping cream. Cover and shake vigorously. Strain into a glass filled with ice. Garnish with whole coffee beans.

SUGARPLUM ROUGE

Makes 6 drinks

1	cup gin, *Tanqueray®*
6	tablespoons frozen lemonade concentrate
¼	cup sugar
1	teaspoon sugar-free peach gelatin powder
½	teaspoon unsweetened tropical punch mix
	Tonic water
	Gumdrops

In a large pitcher, combine gin, lemonade concentrate, sugar, gelatin powder, and punch mix. Stir in 5 cups *water*. Serve in glasses. Add a splash of tonic water to each glass. Garnish with gumdrops.

ANTIPASTO

Start to Finish 15 minutes   **Makes** 8 servings

1	package (5-ounce) mixed salad greens, *Fresh Express®*
1	pound assorted deli meats (such as salami, mortadella, ham, and cappocola)
1	jar (16-ounce) mixed olives, *Giuliano Olive Antipasto®*
1	can (15-ounce) garbanzo beans, rinsed and drained, *Progresso®*
8	ounces fresh mozzarella cheese
4	ounces sliced provolone cheese
2	tomatoes, quartered
1	cup pepperoncini salad peppers
½	to ¾ cup balsamic vinaigrette, *Newman's Own®*

Place salad greens on a cake pedestal or serving platter. Arrange meats, olives, beans, mozzarella cheese, provolone cheese, tomatoes, and pepperoncini on top of greens. Drizzle with vinaigrette.

CRANBERRY KISS

Makes 1 drink

      Ice cubes

2   **ounces Tom Collins drink mix**

2   **ounces cranberry juice**

¾   **ounce spiced rum, *Captain Morgan®***
       Original Spiced Rum

      Fresh spearmint, fresh raspberries

Fill a glass halfway with ice. Add Tom Collins drink
mix, cranberry juice, and rum; stir to combine.
Garnish with spearmint and raspberries.

IRISH EGGNOG

Makes 2 drinks

1	whole egg
1	ounce Irish cream liqueur, *Baileys*®
¼	ounce Irish whiskey, *Bushmills*®
2	cups milk
	Ground nutmeg
	Cinnamon sticks

In a medium bowl, beat together egg, Irish cream liqueur, and Irish whiskey until smooth. Set aside. In a saucepan, bring milk to a boil. Pour over egg mixture, stirring to mix well. Pour into heatproof mugs. Sprinkle each serving with nutmeg. Garnish each mug with a cinnamon stick.

POLAR ESPRESSO

Makes 1 drink

1½	ounces espresso
1	ounce half-and-half
1	ounce white chocolate liqueur, *Godiva*®
½	ounce peppermint schnapps, *Rumple Minze*®
	Ice cubes
	Frozen whipped topping
	Unsweetened cocoa powder

In a cocktail shaker, combine espresso, half-and-half, white chocolate liqueur, and peppermint schnapps. Add ice; cover and shake until very cold. Pour into a chilled martini glass. Garnish with whipped cream and dust with cocoa powder.

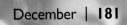

PEAR-Y MERRY MARTINI

Makes 1 drink

Sugar
1½ ounces tequila, *Jose Cuervo® Platino*™
1 ounce pear puree*
1 ounce freshly squeezed lemon juice
¾ ounce sugar syrup
Ice cubes

Wet the rim of a chilled martini glass with *water*. Dip the rim in sugar. In a cocktail shaker, combine tequila, pear puree, lemon juice, and sugar syrup. Add ice; cover and shake until very cold. Pour into prepared glass. ***Note:** For pear puree, blend very ripe pears in a blender or look for bottled pear puree at gourmet food stores.

FESTIVE CHEESE CHIPS

Prep 10 minutes   **Bake** 15 minutes   **Makes** 6 servings

1 bag (5-ounce) potato chips
½ cup white sauce, *Aunt Penny's®*
¼ cup cream cheese, *Philadelphia®*
2 tablespoons crumbled Roquefort cheese
1 tablespoon half-and-half
¼ cup blue cheese crumbles, *Athenos®*

1. Preheat oven to 350 degrees F. Place chips on baking sheet. Bake 15 minutes.

2. In a small saucepan, combine white sauce, cream cheese, Roquefort cheese, and half-and-half. Cook over medium heat until cheese melts, stirring constantly. Remove from heat.

3. Transfer hot chips to serving platter. Drizzle cheese mixture over hot chips. Sprinkle blue cheese crumbles over chips.

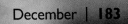

GODIVA TRUFFLETINI

Makes 1 drink

Unsweetened cocoa powder

1   ounce chocolate liqueur, *Godiva*®

½   ounce white chocolate liqueur, *Godiva*®

½   ounce vodka, *Cîroc*®

Ice cubes

Wet the rim of a chilled glass with water. Dip the rim in cocoa powder. In a cocktail shaker, combine remaining ingredients; cover and shake until very cold. Strain into prepared glass.

COFFEE MUG CAKE

Prep 15 minutes   **Bake** 45 minutes   **Stand** 25 minutes
Makes 12 to 16 slices

7   sweet dinner rolls *King's Hawaiian*®

1   box (13.4 ounces) cinnamon swirl quick bread and coffee cake mix, *Pillsbury*®

¾   cup hot water

1   teaspoon instant espresso

¼   cup vegetable oil, *Wesson*®

3   eggs

1   cup whole milk

1   tablespoon sugar, *Domino*®/*C&H*®

Whipped dessert topping, thawed, *Cool Whip*®

Ground cinnamon

Cinnamon sticks

1. Preheat oven to 350 degrees F.

2. *Butter* and *flour* a 10-cup tube pan or square baking dish. Slice 1 inch off tops of rolls. Tear tops into 1-inch pieces; set aside. Place bottoms of rolls, cut sides up, in prepared pan. In a large bowl combine coffee cake batter mix (reserve cinnamon swirl packet), water, instant espresso, oil, and 2 of the eggs. Beat until blended. Pour half of the batter over rolls. Sprinkle with cinnamon swirl.

2. Whisk remaining egg, milk, and sugar in another bowl. Add reserved roll tops to milk mixture; set aside until milk is absorbed. Pour bread mixture over batter in pan, then pour remaining batter on top of bread. Using a skewer or chopstick, swirl batters together.

3. Bake for 45 minutes, or until a toothpick inserted near the center of cake comes out clean.

4. Cool cake in pan on a cooling rack for 25 minutes. Invert cake onto cooling rack; remove pan. Slice and serve warm in coffee mugs. Top with whipped dessert topping and sprinkle with cinnamon. Garnish each with a cinnamon stick.

Index

Masterpiece Mojto In a Collins glass, muddle 2 lime wedges and 1 tablespoon sugar. Add ice. Pour in rum, *Oronoco*®, 2 ounces lime juice, and 2 ounces club soda. Garnish with mint.

Southern Belle In a fluted glass, combine 1 ounce bourbon, *Bulleit®*, and a splash of grenadine. Fill glass with Champagne. Garnish with a cranberry swizzle stick and a lemon twist.

Sandra Lee Semi-Homemade® Cookbook Series

Collect all of these smartly helpful, time-saving, and beautiful books by *New York Times* best-selling author and Food Network star, Sandra Lee.

sandralee.com

Sandra Lee has a passion for simple solutions that create dramatic results in all areas of home life. For exclusive recipes and time- and money-saving tips and tricks to make your home life easier, better, and more enjoyable, log on to www.SandraLee.com. Sign up for the Semi-Homemaker's online club to receive free newsletters filled with fabulous recipes and great entertaining at-home ideas.

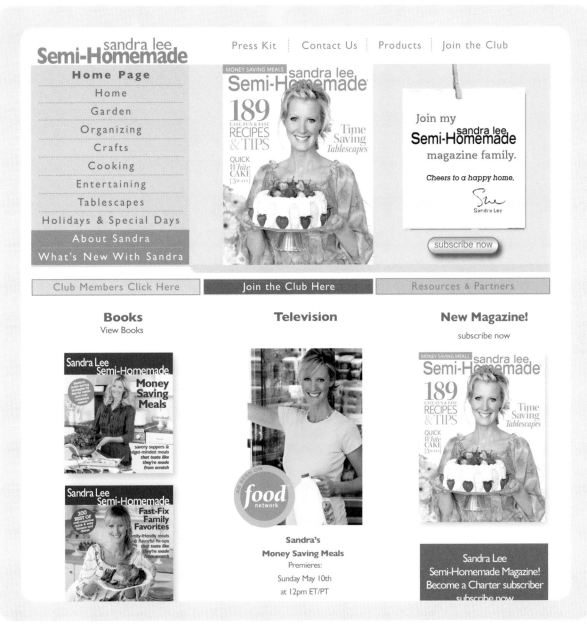

Go to SandraLee.com or Semihomemade.com

Making life easier, better, and more enjoyable